GHOSTS
of the
NORTH

MELANIE WARREN has been involved with the paranormal for fifteen years, prompted by her discovery of the intriguing abilities of a local medium. She is a member of the SPR, and as a trained investigator for ASSAP she has studied a variety of paranormal phenomena, ranging from near-death experiences to alien abduction. She often takes part in ghost-watching vigils in allegedly haunted properties, largely in Lancashire and Cumbria. Melanie has appeared on T.V. several times, and is a regular speaker on Radio Lancashire, where her down-to-earth attitude is popular with listeners. Her broadcasts always result in a flood of phone calls from people who have their own ghostly experiences to tell. She writes regularly for ASSAP's journal, 'Anomaly', contributes articles to 'Prediction' magazine, and in 1994 co-wrote Ghosts of the South West (Broadcast Books) with Tony Wells.

It has been said of TONY WELLS that he has the 'mind of a criminal and the courage of a mouse' – making him ideal for his work as a computer consultant advising banks and institutions on computer security and protection from hackers. This is his third book on the paranormal – as well as co-writing Ghosts of the South-West with Melanie, 1994 saw the publication of Ghostwatching, written with John Spencer (Virgin). He is an active member of both ASSAP and the SPR, spending several evenings a month on ghost-hunting projects with his colleagues. He works with mediums, telepathy experiments and on making 'artificial ghosts' in an attempt to discover the underlying mechanisms behind apparently ghostly phenomena. Tony was also responsible for the instigation of the first evening classes in the UK on the paranormal. He is a regular guest on radio and T.V.

GHOSTS
of the
NORTH

Melanie Warren
and Tony Wells

Broadcast
BOOKS

BRISTOL

A series of ghost stories based on this book was
first broadcast by BBC Radio North in Autumn 1995.

Published by BROADCAST BOOKS
4 Cotham Vale, Bristol BS6 6HR

British Library Cataloguing in Publication Data

A catalogue record for this book is available
from the British Library

ISBN: 1 874092 13 3

Cover designed by Edmund Crewe
Cover photograph by Tony Wells
Text designed and set by Images Publishing Ltd
Printed and bound in Great Britain by Redwood Books Ltd

CONTENTS

ACKNOWLEDGEMENTS

Without the help of many people, this book would certainly have fewer pages, and not quite so much to tell. We have tried to list everyone but apologise if there's anyone we've forgotten: David Hornby, John Whitehead, Phil Pook, Mr and Mrs Armstrong, Mr Stores, Peter Shephard, Mrs Marjorie Johnson, Peter Eyre, Mr C.H. Bagot, Jason Braithwaite, Mr Michael Simpson, Tom and Ann Harrison, Mr John Jebbs, Nigel Holmes, Sue Lloyd, Evelyn Draper, Wally Scott, Billy Mayer, Eddie Benn and Louise Doyle, Bill Montgomery, Shirley Hudson, Mr Ward, Mr Ferguson, Mrs Johnson, Les Bond.

We are indebted to the staff of the following libraries for their prompt and willing assistance: Yorkshire Museum, Scarborough Library, Leeds Library, Darlington Branch Library, Beverley Library, Barrow Library.

Personal thanks are due to the Executive of ASSAP for their continuing support, and also to John and Anne Spencer, for without their encouragement over the last few years, this book and others would not have happened.

We must also thank Zergo Ltd for their tolerance, Kate, Owen, Caz, Matty and the rest of the youth club for their coffee-making duties, Catherine and Lu at Broadcast Books for their enthusiasm and enjoyment of these stories, and June, Penny, Dottie, Sue and Phil for their friendship and encouragement.

INTRODUCTION

Ghosts are alive and well and living in northern England!

When we first started to put together this collection, we knew there were hundreds – thousands – of stories we could choose from. Rather than revamp old stories, we made a point of looking behind the tales and speaking to the people who lived in or near these places of legend. Almost every time, this brought us yet more information – many of the incidents we report have happened in the last five years. Other stories are much older – back through Victorian days, to the witch-hunts of the 1600's, and even further back to medieval times . . .

As well as some tales culled from northern England's rich heritage of legends, we have also spent some time researching real cases, and trying to put them in perspective. We do not attempt to sensationalise or exaggerate these true cases; they are quite disturbing enough on their own. As investigators of the paranormal, who are always seeking out ghosts, we are acutely aware that not everybody feels excited or enthusiastic when they discover a ghost in their own house – especially with the poltergeist type of phenomena. Therefore we hope our readers will understand that we have changed some names and locations to protect people from unwanted publicity. For those who feel they are suffering from such unwelcome visitors, and who would like advice or help in confidence, there are some contact addresses at the end of the book.

MELANIE WARREN AND TONY WELLS

SEPT. 1995

GHOSTLY IMPRESSIONS

There is immense variety in the way hauntings happen – sometimes a ghost will be seen just once and never again, and sometimes it's like living in a horror movie, complete with visual and sound effects. People's reactions differ too – one small incident can frighten a person so much that for the rest of their lives they sleep with the light on, and on the other hand, someone living with an almost daily round of strange rappings and chill breezes will find a method of coping with these peculiarities.

Mrs Hughes of Wallasey remembers how as a girl of 21, she came home from a night out, undressed, switched the light off, got into bed, and almost immediately felt 'something' pulling at the neatly-tucked blankets at the foot of her bed. The sensation lasted for a couple of minutes (though it seemed to last a lot longer) but she eventually managed to shout out at whatever was there. The shout did the trick for the pulling stopped, as suddenly as it had started. Since that time, try as she might, she has not been able to explain it. What really shook her was the fact that her family and friends didn't believe her. They told her that she must have been dreaming, but she knows that this wasn't so, as she had only just climbed into her bed and was nowhere near asleep.

It can be extremely disorientating when you experience a ghost on your own, because it is so hard to convince others that whatever happened was real, at least to you. Certainly it helps if you know that someone has shared your experience . . . as long as they're brave enough to admit it. We have heard several cases where a child has seen a ghost of some kind, and although one of their parents knows that they're telling the truth, because they've seen it too, they tell the child it was just imagining things. Of course such a reaction is understandable, because if you tell your child that you've seen the ghost too, you'll face a barrage of questions about what it is and why it's there – questions for which there are no easy answers.

When Shirley Hudson was a child, she lived in a nineteenth century cottage in Bootle, near Liverpool, sharing a bedroom, and a bed, with her sister. She remembers that when she was eight years old, there was an occasion when she woke up in the middle of the night, and lay still for a while watching the nightlight flickering in the alcove by the door. Suddenly a woman walked into the room. She was a fairly tall woman in her late thirties, with blonde hair piled on top of her head and wearing a blue dressing gown. To Shirley's horror, the woman came across the room and lay down on the bed next to her and her sister. She didn't seem aware of the two little girls at all. Shirley stretched out her hand to touch the woman, but she couldn't feel anything. Shirley tried to scream, but couldn't – in the end she simply turned away, moved as close to the wall as she could and tried to go back to sleep. When she woke in the morning, the woman had gone. Her mother just wouldn't believe her when the story was recounted in the morning. It wasn't until many years later, when everyone had moved out of that house, that her mother admitted she'd had her own share of odd experiences too.

It's easy to understand the reluctance of Shirley's mother to talk about the ghost. How can you explain these things to a child? No one can say for sure what a ghost is, or how or why such phenomena happen. Throughout history people have searched for explanations and in the last hundred years experts all over the world have tried to pigeon-hole these experiences. There are plenty of people who will glibly classify ghosts into categories and explain how these different types of ghosts occur. But as soon as a theory is put forward which seems to explain everything, you can bet that a case will come along which won't fit the theory no matter how hard you wish it would.

There are many different ways of dealing with ghosts too – let's not forget the old standby – hide under the bedclothes and pretend it isn't really happening! Or you might ask the Church to bless the house or to perform an exorcism. You could ask a rescue medium to 'contact the troubled spirit' and ask it to move on. If that doesn't work, there is the other more pragmatic approach. We have heard from a number of doughty northerners that their remedy is to tell the ghosts to 'F*** ***'. Well, it sometimes works!

One of the other frequent things we have come across is that after a ghost sighting the witnesses puzzle over the problem of what exactly happened, and why it happened to them. Was it something to do with them? Was it the house that attracted the ghost? Or did they just happen to be in the wrong place at the wrong time? This is what happened in the example that follows.

Mr Ward moved into a sixty-year-old house near a river, and very soon realised that something was strange about the place. One November night after his wife had gone to bed, he heard footsteps upstairs, and a few moments later his wife appeared looking very white-faced. She told him that the footsteps had not been hers, her room was filled with an unearthly blue mist and she could hear someone breathing heavily in there. The terrified couple dressed hurriedly and went to stay with Mr Ward's mother for the rest of the night.

This seemed to be an example of an 'anniversary ghost', in that the strange things only happened in November every year – for the rest of the year everything was fine. But after four years, the constant footsteps and heavy breathing was becoming annoying, so Mr Ward checked into the history of the house and discovered an interesting story. The previous owner had been a Mrs MacNally, who had worked from it as a prostitute for many years, her customers being American servicemen from the base across the river. Mr Ward also approached a local priest from St Aloysius' Church, expecting him to be dismissive, but instead finding him most sympathetic. The priest explained that he knew the house well – Mrs MacNally in her later years had given up her unsavoury occupation and turned to the church, becoming very religious. She had insisted on a priest from St Aloysius performing a mass in her front bedroom every November, on the Feast of All Souls. Was the blue mist seen by Mrs Ward a 'memory' of incense, used during these masses? The heavy breathing was also explained, when it was discovered that Mrs MacNally had suffered from chronic asthma – in fact, it was this which had led to her death.

The priest arranged to perform an exorcism in the house, and since then everything has been much quieter – not completely quiet, but quieter.

However, not everyone who claims to have a ghost in their house wants to get rid of them. Some families become fond of their ethereal visitors, and regard them almost as pets, giving them nicknames. And some people who see a ghost are scared at first, but later become curious as to the identity of the ghost, and what the story might be behind the haunting.

Mrs Johnson, in Widnes, was fifteen when she saw the ghost of a man in her parents' Victorian house. She was running up the stairs to her room when she saw him, very clearly. He was just standing on the stairs, with one hand resting on the rail, smiling at her. He was wearing very shiny brown boots, and a brown suit. His shirt had a Victorian round collar, his hair was parted in the middle, and he had a moustache. He had a kindly face, and although Mrs Johnson was frightened at first, her brothers soon made her laugh about the incident. 'If you're going upstairs,' they would say, 'ask the man in the brown suit if he's got a ciggy!'

In the years since then, Mrs Johnson has looked into the records, and found that in 1871 her family home was occupied by a gentleman who lived there with his wife, two daughters and four domestic servants. It's difficult, of course, to say if this was the man she saw, but she often wonders about him, and what his life was like. And she is no longer frightened by her experience of meeting him when she was a girl. She thinks there is no reason to be frightened, because as she says: 'He didn't do me any harm.' In fact, it's very unlikely that anyone has ever been physically hurt by a ghost.

As we have said elsewhere in this book, as researchers and investigators we will make a point of walking into supposedly haunted places and seeking out locations where ghosts might be lurking. But this is not always everybody's cup of tea. All the evidence shows that people can be literally terrified when they see a ghost, as the following example shows:

Mr Ferguson used to work at the Dunlop factory in Speke. The factory is next to Speke Hall, which has a legendary White Lady. Perhaps she isn't so legendary after all. Mr Ferguson remembers that one night, a work colleague had to be sedated after driving his truck straight through a woman in white who had appeared out of nowhere in front of him. He jumped off his truck, leaving it running, and ran yelling through the factory, where two of his workmates grabbed him and propelled him towards the factory's medical centre. In cases like this, it's no good saying 'she wasn't really there', because that man would swear that she was . . .

What really frightens people when they see a ghost is that they often do not believe in such things beforehand. They know that if someone else had told them the same story, they would not have believed them – and they know that disbelief is the reaction they can expect from friends, family and colleagues. Nearly everyone who has contributed to this chapter has expressed relief at finally being able to talk to someone who will listen sympathetically to their story. For our part, we have been pleased to include their tales in our collection.

THE GEORGE HOTEL

In March 1993 Tom Harrison and his wife became tenants of the 17th century George Hotel in Preston. They were looking forward to a job they knew they could do well, and to a future in the licensing trade for years to come. Tom was a level-headed, no-nonsense Lancastrian, capable of dealing with any situation, but over the ensuing months his friends, and even his wife Ann, were to begin fearing for his sanity. And even Tom himself began to wonder if he'd lost his grip on reality . . .

The first hint that all was not well in the George came the very first day Tom opened the doors for business. The pub was only a short walk from the local prison, and his first lunchtime customers were a couple of dozen prison officers. Tom was eager to play the congenial host, spotting a possible regular lunchtime trade – things were looking good! But to his dismay, he couldn't pull a single pint from the old-style handpump. The beer was controlled by a switch on the barrel in the cellar below the bar, and as Tom went down to the cellar and switched it on, he cursed himself for not being properly prepared for the lunchtime rush. But when he returned to the bar he found the pump still wouldn't work. Down he went to the cellar again – to find the switch was off . . . he switched it on, returned to the bar . . . still the pump wouldn't work. Several times he repeated this performance, becoming more and more annoyed with every minute – twenty customers standing there waiting for a pint, and he couldn't do anything about it. Eventually the men grew bored with waiting and went to find a pub which did sell beer – leaving Tom standing in his beer cellar bemoaning this small disaster and wondering what on earth he had done wrong.

*The George Hotel. The area shown in this
photograph was once a graveyard*

About two months later, Environmental Health Inspectors announced
that the cobblestoned cellar floor was a safety risk, and would have to
be replaced. Workmen moved in to dig up all the old cobbles, but hit
a problem when they came to a big slab of stone beneath the stairwell;
it couldn't be lifted and in the end had to be smashed and brought out
in pieces. Once in the daylight, someone noticed that there seemed to
be words engraved on the stone – too worn to be legible, but still it
was clear that they had just destroyed a gravestone.

Horrified by this discovery, all work was stopped until a decision
could be taken about what to do next. Why would someone be buried

in the cellar? Should the workmen dig any further down? What might they find? But emotions calmed down when it was realised that a few centuries ago it was entirely legal to bury family members in the gardens or cellars of private property. As the brewery had no wish to dig up anyone's skeleton and face the inevitable fuss this would cause, it was decided just to go ahead and concrete everything over, as originally planned.

Whilst all this work was going on, Tom made many trips down to the cellar, worried about his beer, which was suffering through the vibration from the jackhammers. During one of his inspections, Tom wandered over to where the stone graveslab had laid, and spotted something lying on the surface of the newly uncovered earth. It looked like a ring, blackened with age. Tom took it upstairs to show to Ann. She wasn't impressed, and told him it looked like a metal ring from the top of a bottle, but Tom was certain it was more than that. He cleaned it up, and sure enough he was right – it was a ring, but he'd never seen anything like it before. It was made of gold, and had an embossed inscription running all around it, inlaid with white enamel.

A few days later Tom took the ring to Preston Museum, where a historian deciphered the writing; 'Robert Clay OB 28 Mar 1786 aged 40'. It was a bereavement ring, the historian explained; common enough a couple of centuries ago, made for women to wear when their husbands died. Such rings weren't commonly worn on the hands, though; they were worn around the neck, which explained why the ring was rounded inside, to hang properly on a chain, instead of being flat to fit neatly against a finger. But this was not a bereaved wife's ring, the historian went on – it was a mistress's ring. Usually such rings were decorated with black enamel, the traditional mourning colour, but if the wearer was not married to the one she mourned, she was only allowed to have white enamel. It was also possible to guess that the woman who had owned it was fairly wealthy, as the ring was made from 24 carat gold. Interesting as all this was, Tom thought that now he knew all about the ring's background, it was time to put it away in a safe place and get on with his job.

But down in the cellar, the atmosphere had, literally, changed. Now the cobbles had been lifted the bare earth made the air musty and damp, and that made any place feel spooky. The only odd thing was that Tom's old dog, Basil, who ordinarily followed him everywhere, had taken a sudden dislike to the cellar and now refused to go down there at all. He'd been fine before the work started – in fact Tom and Ann had trouble keeping him out of the beer-room, which had to be kept immaculately clean. But now he wouldn't venture down the cellar steps at all, and would simply wait at the top for Tom to come up again. Very strange. Then another problem arose in the cellar. A horrible, sticky goo had begun to ooze through the whitewashed brickwork. The Estates Manager from the brewery thought it likely that the seepage was coming from a burst drain, which was worryingly unhygienic in a beer cellar. A close look at the old plans of the site showed that the back yard wall had been built directly above the main drain – things were rapidly going from bad to worse! The wall had to be demolished and a deep hole excavated . . . and a few feet down, the workmen found yet another gravestone, but again its surface had deteriorated too badly to tell who it had once commemorated. Once again they had to break the gravestone up to get it out of the way; the pieces were lifted out of the hole and piled up nearby. When the workmen went home that evening, the twelve-foot deep hole was covered with a board. The night that followed was to be the most terrifying night of Tom's life.

In the early hours of the morning Tom and Ann were awakened

by banging and thumping noises coming from the rooms above. Tom thought it must be his eldest son getting up and ready for work, but there was no need for all that racket. Doors were being opened and loudly closed – why was he banging around from room to room? Tom sat on the edge of the bed and resolved to give him a good telling-off about consideration for other people, when he came downstairs. There were a few more slams, and then he heard footsteps thudding down the stairs, and out of the corner of his eye caught a shadow going into the room opposite the bedroom. He called out, 'Alan – is that you?' But there was no answer. Tom stood up and walked round the bed, reaching the door to see a form leaving the room and going into another. He heard another loud bump, and shouted more angrily, 'Alan! Come here!' Then he sensed that someone was standing behind him – he turned, expecting to see Alan or another member of his family – but found himself face to face with a man he had never seen before in his life. The stranger stared straight at him and said, 'Don't you ignore me.' With that, he passed by Tom, who was rigid with shock, and went down the stairs, followed by Basil, the dog.

Tom later described the stranger as a big man, standing about six feet tall, with long thin features, intense eyes, and with a short-cut beard. He was wearing a long black coat and hat, black pants, and a shirt with a square-cut white collar which made him look like a Quaker. The sight of this very oddly-dressed man so shocked Tom that he stood quite still for some seconds – until he heard the vestibule door downstairs bang shut – it was a heavy old door on a pressure spring and it made a very distinctive sound. The noise brought Tom back to his senses. He ran downstairs to look for Basil.

Reaching the bottom of the stairs, he found that the vestibule door was locked – from the inside – well, of course it was, he always made sure it was locked, every night, before he went to bed. What's more, the door was alarmed – if anyone had really left the building through that door, the alarm would have been triggered. Yet he had definitely heard the door bang shut – what was going on? And where had Basil disappeared to?

That was even more puzzling. Basil, it turned out, was in the pub – behind yet another locked door. Tom stood and fumbled with the key, but listening to Basil howling beyond the door and having to deal with this inexplicable situation was too much for him. Whether it was simply fear, he didn't know, but he suddenly felt an unaccountable chill, and turned and ran upstairs to the bedroom, leaving the poor dog where he was. A few minutes passed whilst Tom tried to gather his senses, then he went back downstairs, unlocked the door, and let Basil out. Basil hurtled up to the bedroom and hid in a corner, obviously as confused as Tom by what had just happened.

Until now, Ann had been very sceptical of the things Tom said had been happening in the pub. Even that night, she wondered if he had simply been downing too much of his own beer ! But she too had heard the sound of the vestibule door slam shut, and she had seen how scared Tom was, and she had seen the reaction of the poor dog. She tried to persuade Tom to come back to bed, but there was no way he could go back to sleep just yet. There was a fire escape leading from their bedroom, so he decided to sit out there for a while and smoke a cigarette while he calmed down.

By now it was about five o'clock in the morning. Trying to make sense of what had happened was unsettling, and Tom smoked his roll-up nervously. Down in the back yard he heard a dull thud, and registered the fact that the back-yard gate had just been closed. But by whom, at this time in the morning? He glanced down at the back-yard wall and gate . . . and it suddenly hit him that he was seeing something

23

that wasn't there – the workmen had demolished the wall, hadn't they? But he could still see it quite clearly! Then he realised that the whole landscape was different – the back yard was cobbled, and there was a road running beyond the yard wall, and on the other side of the street were a few buildings, most noticeably a shop which sold candles; there was a light on in the room above the shop, and he could see a man pacing about in front of the window. And a little further down the street was a woman in a long old-fashioned dress, walking her dog – as Tom watched in amazement, she left the dog outside the candle-shop and disappeared inside, to reappear a few moments later in the upstairs room, where she stabbed the man . . . came out again, collected her dog and calmly walked away. Tom dashed back into the bedroom and woke Ann. He sat on the edge of the bed, white with shock, and told his astounded wife the whole story. He begged her to believe him, insisting that he had never been as much in earnest as he was now.

It might all have been easier for Tom to understand if he could have seen some link between his altercation with the man in the house and the murder he had just seen enacted, but as he lay in bed trying to get to sleep he knew they were not connected, and that just made it worse. Why was he hallucinating like this? Was he finally losing his mind?

He managed to sleep for a little while, and when he woke and looked out of the window again, everything was back to normal. Or so he thought. When the workmen arrived to carry on their digging in the back yard, they came into the pub and demanded an explanation for what they had just found. The pieces of the gravestone, which they had left in a pile, had been put back together, on top of the board which covered the deep hole. Who could have done it? The younger children hadn't been allowed to play outside the night before because it had been raining, and no one else had access to the area behind the pub.

They decided there had to be a logical explanation, and it was better not to worry about it. The workmen moved the gravestone pieces and piled them up again, and carried on putting in a new drain, and that evening Tom locked the back door and told his children that the yard was dangerous and on no account were they to go out there. But the next morning, the stone pieces were back on top of the board again; this time evenly spaced out around the edges. There was no explanation. Tom told the builders to put the pieces back in the hole where they had come from, and cover them up. It seemed that was where they wanted to be.

Meanwhile, down in the cellar, other people were finding that things were distinctly odd. There was a CD player down there which fed music to the bar, and the CDs were kept in a turntable storage unit. A few times Tom would go down and find discs lying on the floor, and one day another member of staff came running upstairs, scared out of his wits, because he had just seen discs flying out of the storage unit all by themselves. The beerpump was forever switching itself off, and one day Tom found himself shouting at whoever it was who was interfering with it; 'Will you leave these beer-barrels alone, you! You're getting on my nerves!' To his horror, he was answered by a deep, unearthly laugh, 'Ha ha ha ha!' Tom was out of that cellar in a moment.

Then things started happening in the bar itself. The bar-flap was often propped up against the wall, for easy access to the bar, and as it was a heavy slab of wood it couldn't move even if it was shaken. On several occasions customers were astonished to see it banging itself against the wall. Quite a few customers left and never came back . . .

One evening a man came up to Tom and told him he'd better

check the Gents' toilets, because he could hear someone in there kicking down one of the cubicle doors. Tom shot in there, ready for action, and he could see the door banging – but nothing else.

Another evening Tom and Ann heard the sounds of a woman, crying, coming from the corridor which led to the toilets. Thinking that some poor girl was being attacked, Tom, ran into the corridor to see one of his regular customers being held against the wall . . . and her feet were a few inches off the floor. Tom could see that it was his old friend the man in the black coat who was holding her aloft, but the poor girl couldn't see anything, and she was petrified. 'There's somebody holding me!' she screamed. Tom ran to tackle the man as he would any human assailant, and the girl dropped to the ground.

The fact that other people were witnessing the weird things that happened in the pub made Tom feel slightly better – perhaps he wasn't going mad after all – but clearly things couldn't go on like this. Stories were going around about the George, and business was suffering.

An elderly customer had mentioned that if Tom and Ann wanted the place investigated in a spiritualist context, she knew an excellent medium who might be able to help. Tom had declined, saying he didn't believe in all that mumbo-jumbo. But now he was beginning to think it might be worth a try. Ann rang the number they had been given, and arranged for the medium to pay a visit.

When she arrived, the medium wandered around the building and seemed to know instinctively which parts of the pub were affected. Downstairs in the cellar, she picked out a very small room which was used as the bottle-room and had concrete, not cobbled, flooring. She was sure that at one time this had been a staircase and that there was another cellar beneath . . . later, the records showed that she was right.

Then the medium said that there were two young women buried

26

down in the hidden cellar. But she wasn't at all happy with the atmosphere in the place, and despite her long experience as a medium, she told Tom and Ann that if they wanted a seance to exorcise the spirit causing the trouble, this was not something she could handle on her own. There was far too much disturbance.

Tom and Ann talked it over. They had already been approached by another brewery to run a different pub, and were due to take up their new posts in a matter of weeks. They would be out and away from the George – but how could they leave the new tenants to face what they had been living with for six months? Tom had lost an awful lot of weight and couldn't sleep – he didn't want to leave his successor to the same fate. They decided to go ahead with a seance.

On the appointed night, the medium turned up with two other women, and a young man. Together with Tom and Ann, they positioned themselves in the parlour lounge, one of the oldest parts of the George. Then the medium explained what they were going to do. Quite simply, Robert Clay, who was commemorated on the bereavement ring Tom had found, didn't know he was dead. The purpose of the evening was to summon his spirit, and tell it to go towards the light, but as Tom seemed to be the focus for this spirit, she told him to sit quite still, and on no account to move, as there was every chance the spirit would try to 'possess' him. Terrifying.

As the seance progressed, Tom began to feel under intense pressure – he felt as if someone was trying to push him in the back, very hard – he remembered what the medium had told him and tried to stay still, but found that he was rocking backwards and forwards under the pressure – and then the pressure lifted, and he saw that the young man's face opposite him was changing. His features were melting and reforming into the face of a totally different man who looked directly at Tom. It was the man with the intense, thin face he had seen that terrible night of banging and disturbances, the man who had said 'Don't you ignore me!'

Almost terrified out of his wits, Tom looked at the other two women, and saw that their faces were also changing. They became younger and younger, until he found himself gazing at two teenagers who were obviously frightened of the man opposite Tom, who was Robert Clay. And the story came out that Robert Clay had abused and murdered these two women, and buried their bodies in the cellar. Robert Clay had suffered enormous guilt over his actions, and so had continued to haunt the building; his apparently threatening order to Tom, 'Don't you ignore me', was simply his way of getting his story out, so that he might find forgiveness and peace at last.

The atmosphere in the parlour lounge was very tense; the women were crying, and the young man was clearly frightened by what was happening to him. The medium repeated again and again to Robert Clay and the two young women that they must go towards the light, and Tom watched in awe as the far wall began to emit a cloudy glow, and the two small figures of the women walked away from the mediums and went into the light. And then, with relief, he saw the figure of Robert Clay leave the young man and also disappear into the luminous cloud.

Tom only saw Robert Clay once more; but this was after he had moved into his new pub! One night he looked up from the bar to see Robert Clay standing there in front of him, but this time he didn't look at all threatening, in fact he was smiling, and after a few seconds he just faded away. As for the bereavement ring; after the seance, the medium told Tom he should always wear it, saying that it would protect him. He wears it to this day, on a gold chain round his neck. He's been told it's worth quite a bit, but he won't sell it. But he didn't give much credence to the idea that it would protect him . . . until he went on a deep-sea fishing trip. Forty miles out to sea, with seven-foot waves lashing the boat, Tom got a bite and was dragged over the side. He sank like a stone, but never for a moment thought he was going to die, despite the fact that he was wearing all his heaviest fishing gear and could see the bottom of the boat getting further and further away. Suddenly he felt as if someone had put a strong arm around him and he was on his way back to the surface. He broke the surface with a smile on his face.

It may interest the reader to know that Tom and Ann did some extensive checking of the records, with the assistance of the Historian at Preston Museum. Amongst other things, they discovered that the graves found on their property were not unusual; at one time the whole of Church Street had been a burial ground for the Parish Church, a few hundred yards away. But unfortunately, they couldn't find Robert Clay anywhere in the records, despite having the indisputable proof of his existence in the form of his mistress' bereavement ring. They searched for a record of his death – after all, they knew the exact date – but it was just not there. They knew he was forty when he died, so they counted back forty years and checked for evidence of his birth – again, they found nothing. However, there was only one Clay family in Preston at the time, and whilst Robert was not amongst the names, there was one family member whose age suggested that he may well have been Robert Clay's father, and who happened to be in charge of the House of Correction – situated directly opposite the George.

If Robert Clay was a murderer, and if his father really did run the House of Correction, it actually makes sense that Robert's name cannot be found in any official records. In those days, before the official Census came into force, if someone committed a heinous crime, their family could arrange to have his or her name excised from the records completely.

But there was still one piece of the jigsaw missing. What of the murder in the candle shop? This had not involved Robert Clay in any way, but during their researches Tom and Ann discovered that there was indeed a chandlers on that very site, and that a murder had been committed there . . . but the trauma of having cleared up one murder mystery was quite enough for them, for the moment . . .

THE POLTERGEIST
OF LUCAS ROAD

From the outside, the haunted house at Lucas Road seemed quite ordinary. Lucas Road was in an unremarkable town in the county of Durham. The street had its share of problems – not enough work for some of the folk, and maybe a little too much rowdiness on a Friday night – nothing unusual in an area where the hard pattern of working life centred on the local pit – traditional work that had absorbed generations of men in the area and which is now, of course, a past memory. But the occupants of the house in question have a very unusual story to tell.

Paul and Mary Clayton had moved into the house in 1965. They were a young couple, not long married, with a baby son, Brian, named after Mary's grandfather. Their lives were full of organising their home and caring for the baby. But by the time Brian was two, Mary was hankering to go back to work. She missed the company of her friends at the biscuit factory, and the extra money would pay for a new kitchen and all the other things she was keen to do to the house. Mary's parents were quite happy to look after Brian during the day, and this was very convenient as their house was only a few streets away.

Mary saved her earnings carefully, and soon they were able to begin work on the new kitchen. The builders took a week to demolish the wall between the tiny back room and the small kitchen, so making a larger, more comfortable room. It was a terribly messy job, but in a couple more weeks the new cabinets would have been fitted, and the new floor laid. They were resigned to the mess, and Mary was looking forward to cooking the Christmas dinner for her whole family when it was finished.

One winter's evening, just after the kitchen cabinets had been installed, Paul's factory had a problem with the machinery and so they let the workforce home a few hours early. Paul called straight round to Mary's parents to pick up Brian but nobody was in – he guessed that all three were in the local park. So he went back home, looking forward to quiet hour or two with a brew in front of the television.

As soon as he opened the front door, Paul knew something was wrong but he couldn't place what exactly it was. There was just a funny feeling in the house. As he closed the front door behind him, he also noticed a funny smell, like burnt cabbage. But that meant Mary must have rushed home at lunchtime, put some cabbage on to cook, then gone back to work and forgotten all about it. That didn't make any sense at all. He went straight into the kitchen to find the source of the smell, expecting to find a blackened pan on the stove. But he certainly didn't expect the sight that confronted him. All the cupboards has been emptied out onto the kitchen floor. The place was awash with broken glass, cornflakes, milk, flour, and dented cans. It was a terrible sight.

Paul's first thought was that the house had been burgled. Knowing what Mary's reaction might be, he ran through the house to appraise himself of any other wreckage and to see what might have been taken. After a frenzied examination, he began to relax a little. There were no other obvious signs of damage, and nothing actually appeared to have been stolen. He examined the back door and other places of entry and couldn't see any way a burglar could have got into the house without forcing a way in. All was secure. So how did the kitchen come to be wrecked?

Paul called the police, and when the constable arrived, he was just as puzzled. He confirmed that there was no forced point of entry, and couldn't understand why nothing had been taken. As Paul had expected, he also wasn't very encouraging about the possibility of catching the culprits. But he was sympathetic, and offered to stay until Mary got home, to help break the bad news.

There was no doubt in Mary's mind, when she returned that evening, that they had had burglars, and she was very upset. Then she became quite frightened about the whole affair, and for several weeks talked of moving out of the house entirely. The foul smell persisted despite everything she did – she was sure it was a spiteful prank by the intruders, to have hidden some rotting garbage somewhere it couldn't be found.

But the family's ordeal wasn't over yet.

Ten days later, Paul got an urgent phone call at work from his neighbour June. It seemed that there was the sound of banging and crashing and the shattering of glass coming from their house. Paul, hopeful that they might catch the burglars red-handed, asked her to phone the police, while he asked his foreman for a few hours off.

He drove furiously across town to his house and to his relief found a policeman outside. It was the same one who called round the last time, and so there was no need for explanations. As they stood outside, they could both hear the noises of doors banging and glass crashing. Without a word Paul opened the door with his key and let the constable in first. Paul followed him into the hallway and up the stairs, as the sounds were coming from the top of the house. He was so intent on getting the perpetrators who were invading his house that it wasn't until nearing the top landing that he again noticed the intense burnt vegetable smell. This time the smell was so bad that he nearly vomited. He fought the sensation and rushed onto the landing. Suddenly, the noise stopped.

Once on the top landing Paul found the policemen looking puzzled, with his head to one side, standing in the bedroom doorway. Not sure what was going on Paul pushed past him to confront the now quiet burglars and found nothing. He did a double take, and checked the two other rooms. Nothing at all was out of place. There was no obvious reason for the noises that they had all heard . . .

As can be imagined, Mary was almost beside herself. The effect this peculiar incident had on the household was to impose further strain – Mary was now threatening to take Brian and move temporarily back to her parents house. Paul, as well as having to support Mary, was finding it difficult to sleep, for he was constantly mentally replaying the event, trying to find an explanation for the sounds that they had all heard, which seemed to have no physical cause.

Three days later the next incident occurred, and again with witnesses. It was a Saturday morning and Paul had his workmate Alan round to help him with a plumbing problem in the kitchen. Mary had taken Brian to her parents while the water was disconnected. This problem had been caused by Paul in the first place, as a direct result of the awful smells. In an attempt to find the cause, Paul had checked the kitchen sink waste pipe. He had found it remarkably easy to dismantle, but when reassembled, it leaked.

Alan was under the sink with a wrench, tightening up the joints, with Paul outside in the garden holding a section of the pipe still. Suddenly there was a loud 'POP' and then a curse as Alan bumped his head under the sink cupboard. Paul rushed into the kitchen to find Alan upright, rubbing his head and looking at the kitchen worksurface – which was now covered in brown sauce. The cause of the POP was plain to see. The bottle had exploded; the pressure inside it had actually caused the bottle-top to embed itself in the polystyrene ceiling. Paul stared at the bottle and the mess in the kitchen, and then jumped as one of the kitchen cupboard doors swung open gently and a packet of Rice Krispies tipped over, spilling its contents over the floor. They both looked at each other and then Paul bolted out of the back door, with Alan following close behind.

Alan refused to set foot in the house again and it was about this time that friends and family started to use the word poltergeist in connection with the incidents – which were beginning to get more and more destructive. The crunch came about a month later when Paul, Mary and Brian had a particularly bad night; for several hours it sounded like a herd of elephants was running around the bedroom next door, the landing and the rooms below. Paul checked many times, but as soon as he got out of bed to investigate the noises stopped. That night was the last straw and Mary went to the local vicar for help. After some questioning of the family, the vicar decided to perform an exorcism, but he insisted that no family members should attend, only himself and a fellow cleric to assist him.

At four p.m. on a windy December afternoon, the exorcism took place, while Paul, Mary and Brian stayed with their next door neighbours. After an hour of waiting they were all beginning to wonder what was going on. Paul even put a wine glass to the partition wall to see if he could hear what was happening, but heard nothing.

In the end, they waited for a total of four hours before the vicar called round to say the exorcism was complete. The vicar would not reveal what had happened, but seemed satisfied that the exorcism had worked. The awful smell was gone. In fact, subsequent visitors remarked on how pleasant the house now was – no odd smells, not a hint of burnt cabbage.

From that day, Paul and Mary suffered no more awful incidents. Brian eventually grew up and went his own way in life, moving out at age of twenty five to be married to a girl from London where they started their own life. Paul and Mary, now grandparents themselves, still live in the house which once gave them such a terrifying time. They seem none the worse for their strange experience, although Paul does still occasionally tease Mary about her insistence on having air-fresheners in every room, just in case . . .

THE CAULD LAD OF HYLTON

Hylton Castle, near Sunderland in Durham, dates from 1072, but now it stands in ruins. Little more than the gateway still remains. But at the beginning of the seventeenth century it was the home of Sir Robert Hylton, the local Baron. Hylton Castle had been his family home for three hundred years. It was also the scene of a most cruel murder, which, if the stories are to be believed, was the cause of a haunting which lasted for almost a century . . .

One evening, Sir Robert paced about impatiently at the entrance to the castle, waiting for his stable-lad, young Roger Skelton, to saddle his horse and bring it to him, as instructed. Finally the ill-tempered Baron could stand it no longer – he marched round to the stables, intent on discovering the cause of the delay, only to find the stable-lad fast asleep in a bed of straw. Thoroughly enraged by this show of wilful disobedience, not to mention downright laziness, the Baron picked up a hayfork and stabbed the young boy. Then, realising that in his temper he had dealt a fatal blow, he covered young Roger's body with straw and left it there until nightfall, when he dragged it to a deep pond nearby, and threw the body in.

The facts are recorded in the documents from a coroner's inquest, in 1609, when Sir Robert Hylton was tried for murder. The Baron was found guilty – but as a body was not recovered, he was later able to procure a complete pardon. But it seems the ghost of Roger Skelton found this an unsuitable verdict, as he chose to haunt the castle kitchens from then on, in a rather disturbing manner. He could often be heard, sobbing and wailing outside the castle walls at night. When he was seen, he was stark naked – it was this fact which earned him the nickname of 'The Cauld Lad'. There are reputed to be numerous sightings of the Cauld Lad. One was as recently as 1970, when a miner coming home from his night shift at the local pit heard someone shout to him from the ruined castle walls. In the next instant, a figure appeared beside him and kept pace with him, no matter how fast the terrified miner ran. When he reached his front door, the figure vanished . . . but when the miner looked out through his front window he saw the figure return to his front door, and stay there motionless for many hours.

An early print of Hylton Castle before the alterations of 1863.

But the Cauld Lad of legend was not so much a ghost as a poltergeist, who chose to perform helpful tasks in the dead of night, as a 'Brownie'. Like these helpful domestic goblins, he took pride in putting things in order, would prepare food for next day, wash utensils, and stack plates. Late at night, the servants who slept in the Great Hall would hear him hard at work in the kitchens, but the kitchen staff found that if they should retire to bed with no tasks left undone, the ghost would show his displeasure by breaking crockery, mixing powdered goods such as sugar and salt together, emptying ashes into the flour bin and generally going berserk – so they soon learned to leave some jobs for him to do.

The Cauld Lad was also good at scaring those servants who imagined they could steal a little food and get away with it; one poor servant girl, finding herself alone in the dairy, went to take a crafty drink from the cream and was startled to hear a disembodied voice chastising her, saying; 'Ye sip, and ye sip, and ye sip, but ye never give the Cauld Lad a sip!'

However, helpful as the Cauld Lad could be, it was disconcerting to have a brownie around the place. Eventually, as a last resort, the staff decided to try a traditional way of getting rid of him, by making some clothes for him to wear. A cloak and a hood in the finest quality Lincoln green was carefully fashioned and stitched and when it was finished, the kitchen staff left it for the Cauld Lad, hiding themselves away to see what would happen. At midnight, the Cauld Lad duly appeared, and put on the cloak with obvious delight. He danced around the kitchen all night in his glee, and then, at cockcrow, everyone present heard him say; 'Here's a cloak and here's a hood – the Cauld Lad of Hylton will do no more good!' And with that, he disappeared, and life in the kitchen returned to normal.

Maybe it *was* the cloak which finally laid Roger Skelton to his rest – but it is on record that in 1703, almost a hundred years after Roger's death, the local pond was drained and the skeleton of a young man was discovered. It was given a decent Christian burial, after which, as one would expect, there were far fewer reports of ghostly happenings. Though even today people sometimes report the sounds of wailing, coming from the castle ruins, late at night . . .

Hylton Castle today, shrouded in mists rising from the River Wear.

Only 500 yards from Hylton Castle, there's a pub called 'The Cauld Lad', named after the legendary boy. The castle may not be haunted any longer, but at the pub, it's a different story. The 'Cauld Lad' was built in the 1960's, and stands on what was originally castle ground. Mrs Armstrong has worked at the pub for ten years, first as a barmaid and then, with her husband, as proprietor. During those ten years she, and the other pub staff, have grown quite used to the odd events which regularly happen around the place. Keys go missing, things are moved, there are strange smells, and often a member of staff will have the unsettling sensation of someone standing behind them.

Several times a month something odd will happen, mainly in the cellar and the lounge, and not only at night – just as often these things happen in broad daylight. The staff pay little attention to these occurrences, saying that 'after a while, you just get used to it . . . ' And certainly the occurrences aren't very frightening – just inconvenient – most of the time.

On some occasions, however, things can get a little more unsettling. Such was the experience Mrs Armstrong had, late one night, as she was checking the day's takings in a small safe-room, down in the cellar. Quite suddenly, she felt the atmosphere in the cellar change. Over the years she had grown quite used to the feelings of the place, but this was different. What she was feeling now was so disturbing that she began to shake, quite involuntarily. She had the distinct feeling that if she stayed where she was, she would see something she didn't want to see. Needless to say, she got out fast!

The cellar was also regarded with suspicion by a barman once employed at the pub, who wouldn't venture down there without the family dog, who was a comforting cross between a Rottweiler and an Alsatian. This fearsome-looking creature was, in fact, a very well-behaved and placid dog, and usually she would go down to the cellar quite happily – but sometimes she would erupt in an energetic bout of barking and growling for no obvious reason. After some minutes of this, she would always run up the stairs and into the lounge, where she would run around the tables like a mad thing, refusing to be calmed by her concerned owners.

Mrs Armstrong had no idea what – or who – could be causing such distress to her dog (and her barman), and she tended not to think about these episodes once they were over. But one evening, she was standing at the bar in the lounge, chatting to an interesting couple who were just passing through the area, when she noticed the woman had suddenly turned deathly pale. She was silently staring at a spot beyond Mrs Armstrong, where it became apparent she had seen something no one else had seen. She explained that her attention had been taken by a man in a grey suit, who was there one moment – and gone the next. Is the strange atmosphere in the pub his doing? And if so, why?

One last interesting story is told by Mrs Baker, the pub's regular cleaner, who comments that often when she has mopped the floor, she comes back to it to see footprints running through it. A child's footprints. Naked footprints. Could it be . . . the Cauld Lad himself? We have no evidence that this is the case, but it's a good example of how legends grow up. After all, the particular wings of Hylton Castle which were once home to the Cauld Lad's ghost no longer exist, and the pub is only a few hundred yards away; it's logical, even if deplorably unscientific, to assume that the ghost has simply moved house . . .

THE GHOST OF TWEED STREET

Eddie Benn, a man now in his mid-forties, is a firm believer in ghosts. When he was only a boy of nine, he had to spend a night with his family in a haunted house. Their experiences that night were more than enough to convince them all of the existence of the supernatural.

This story is unusual, for both Eddie and his mother approached us completely independently. As investigators we found this fascinating, for although there were some minor variations in detail, the content of both their accounts was very similar. This is the story as told to us by Eddie, and we have made only minor changes to his words.

The haunted house was a rented terraced house in Tweed Street, in the south end of Liverpool. Eddie's Aunt Lizzie lived there for many years, quite peacefully and with no hint of anything supernatural. The only strange thing about the place was her lodger, Mr Haddington. He was a middle-aged chap who seemed a bit eccentric and rather anti-social. He mostly kept himself to himself, as his room upstairs was set up as a bedsitter, but he did come down to share the front room with Aunt Lizzie from time to time. He was interested in astronomy and all sorts of other odd things, but he wasn't very friendly. When the rest of the family came to visit, he always made it clear that he didn't find their presence welcome.

Housing was scarce in the 1950's because of the bombing that had flattened large areas of Liverpool during the war. So when Eddie's Uncle Bobby and his wife were having problems finding accommodation, Aunt Lizzie offered to let them live with her for a while. It was a bit cramped, but everyone got along fine – until Aunt

Lizzie died. Then things between Bobby and Mr Haddington became tense. Bobby would have liked him to leave, but the lodger had no intention of moving out. They eventually settled into an uneasy partnership in the house, and tried to get along as best they could.

One evening, Bobby and his wife and Mr Haddington were all in the front room, when suddenly Mr Haddington began muttering to himself. He turned to Bobby and said, 'The spirits are around us . . . ' Bobby was a sensible down-to-earth Scouser who had no time for any of that sort of stuff, and he told Mr Haddington so, in no uncertain terms. Mr Haddington got to his feet and disappeared upstairs to his room in a temper.

Next morning, Bobby's wife insisted that he should take Mr Haddington a cup of tea and his paper, by way of an apology. Reluctantly Bobby went upstairs with tea and the paper, but when he knocked on Mr Haddington's door he got no answer. He opened the door and saw that their lodger was sitting in a big wing-chair, facing him. He was stark naked and stone dead, staring straight ahead. The inquest decided his death was due to natural causes, but it still seemed a strange way to die.

For a while after their lodger died, Bobby said that strange things were happening in the house from time to time, but no one paid much attention. They put it down to Bobby's imagination, pricked by his conscience about the way he had spoken to the old man before he died. It was that which was making him imagine that Mr Haddington was still there, haunting his last home . . .

After a long wait, Bobby's application for a house in Kirkby came through, and he offered his old house in Tweed Street to Eddie's parents. They accepted gratefully, for at that time they, Eddie and his two small brothers were sharing a house with their grandmother. The extra space would be most welcome. The day Bobby moved out, Eddie and his family were all set to move in.

Eddie remembers that the moment he set foot in the house, the hairs on the back of his neck stood up. It was impossible to ignore the feeling of not being welcome there, as if someone or something was saying 'Get out! Get out!' He stood at the bottom of the stairs and watched his Dad go up to the landing. Then the door opposite Dad slammed shut in his face . . . he came back down those stairs very fast, using language he shouldn't have done in front of a nine-year-old boy.

While Dad was busy sorting out the van, Eddie and his brother were helping their Mum in the kitchen. It was impossible to feel they were alone in the house. Something banged on the ceiling, twice, followed by sounds from upstairs as if someone were frantically looking in drawers for a lost object, then getting bad-tempered because the drawers wouldn't close again. They all heard the noises, yet they knew that there was no one up there. When Dad came back, he went upstairs to investigate, but said there was nothing there, and nothing had been moved . . .

That night, the whole family went to bed. Not surprisingly they decided they would all sleep in the same room, the main bedroom at the front of the house. The atmosphere was not pleasant, but things seemed quiet enough, and everyone tried to settle down for a night's sleep. Suddenly Eddie's Mum jumped with fright. 'What's that?' she shouted. Up in the corner of the room, near the ceiling, there was a small but vivid blue light. None of the family had seen anything like it before. From the room next door came the sounds of someone rummaging through drawers again. The atmosphere grew decidedly uncomfortable. By now everyone was out of bed, wanting to see what could possibly be making those noises.

Mum went downstairs, and as Dad was about to start down after her, all the upstairs doors slammed shut at once. Worse was to follow. Mum then got the distinct impression that there was someone standing in the doorway of the front room. She couldn't exactly make out the shape, but she knew there was someone, or something there. She was also getting the feeling that she should gather her family and get out immediately!

When the morning eventually came, everything was quiet again, but that one night had been enough for everyone. They packed their things and moved as fast as they could back to Grandma's. Later that day Mum had to go back to the house to collect a few things which had been overlooked in the rush, but she was dreading going back there. A relative offered to go with her, a no-nonsense kind of woman who was not the sort to be bothered by anything unusual. But when she reached the house, she stopped at the front door and wouldn't go any further. Like everyone else, she had the distinct feeling that someone was standing at the bottom of the stairs, outside the front room – someone who didn't want company.

After the night spent in the house by Eddie and his family, people were more inclined to listen to the stories Bobby had been telling about the place for many years. There was one story that Eddie remembered very well. Bobby had once held a party at the house in Tweed Street, and one of his mates, a big strong man, had gone out to the yard to use the lavatory. He walked down the path, following an old lady, idly wondering who she was. He stopped in amazement when he saw her disappear through the toilet door – without opening it first! The chap fled the house and refused to go there ever again.

The house in Tweed Street is no longer there; like so much of Liverpool it has been demolished to make way for better houses and office buildings. But neither Eddie nor his Mother will ever forget the place, and how the atmosphere – or was it Mr Haddington's ghost? – managed to keep everyone away.

AN ANTIQUE GHOST

In 1981 John Jebb retired from his post as a CID Officer with Merseyside Police and was finally able to fulfil his dream of running his own antique shop. The little shop in Churchtown seemed perfect. Like many of the buildings in this ancient village near Southport, it was a thatched cottage, hundreds of years old, and with many charming features. Behind the plasterboard were the original wattle and daub walls, and upstairs you could see that the roof had been made from whole trees – their winding branches were still visible in the ceiling. It was a delightful place and John and his wife both fell in love with it. But when he bought the shop, John didn't expect to take on a resident ghost.

The previous owner had mentioned quite casually that if he ever heard someone knocking on the wall, not to worry – it would only be the ghost – and if he told it to be quiet and go away, it would. But this was not the sort of advice a sensible ex-policeman was going to take seriously!

One day, however, he and his wife did indeed hear something which sounded just like someone knocking on the wall dividing the two rooms in the shop. There was no one on the other side, no one who could be knocking. Perhaps it was just the vagaries of the plumbing? Or something to do with the aged construction of the wall, expanding as the day warmed up? The knocking continued, and John and his wife looked at each other, remembering what the last owner had said. At last John said out loud, 'Please be quiet and go away!' And the knocking stopped.

It was easy enough to call this one occurrence an amusing coincidence. Indeed it was amusing, when the knockings occurred on later occasions, to be able to stop them by telling them to be quiet. But as time passed other things happened which weren't so easily cured. About a year later, John was alone in the shop late one afternoon when he heard a clattering sound above his head. At first he thought that children must be passing on their way home from school and throwing empty cans or bottles onto the low roof of the shop. But then he realised the roof was thatched – bottles would have a soft landing – the clattering must be coming from the room upstairs. He went upstairs and found that some wooden chairs, which he was sure he had placed in a line against a wall, were now lying on their backs all over the floor, just as if someone had been throwing them about the room. He couldn't explain it – so he set the chairs upright again, and tried to forget about it.

Months passed quietly, with only the odd knocking to disturb the peace of the shop – and that was easy enough to handle. John would tell it to stop, and it did. Then one day John's daughter popped in with a school-friend. The two girls went through to the kitchen at the rear of the shop, and a few seconds later John heard a piercing scream. He ran to see what had happened, and found his daughter's friend white-faced with fear, swearing that someone had grabbed her shoulder – but there was no one standing behind her! She ran from the shop in terror and refused to visit again. This was rather less amusing than the harmless raps and knocks.

Despite his sensible nature, John began to wonder if his charming little shop really was haunted. There seemed to be no other explanation for some of the things that had happened, although the very idea of a ghost went against the grain for a man with his experience and training. The next question was, who was doing the haunting?

Little Thatch Antiques Shop in Churchtown.

In the summer of 1984, an explanation began to unfold. John was chatting to a friend who had popped into the shop – a female friend who had always claimed to be 'sensitive' to the paranormal. In mid-sentence she stopped talking, and her face went pale. She told John that she could see a little old woman standing next to him. She described the woman as being very small, about four feet eleven, and wearing an old-fashioned bonnet and a full-length black dress with a pinafore over the top. Was this the ghost who had caused such a nuisance?

Things were quiet for several months, apart from the occasional rapping noise, which John had grown used to by now. But then one day something really spectacular happened, witnessed by John, his wife, and a customer and his young son who had come into the shop to examine a train set. The boy was on the floor watching the train go round the track, John was chatting to the lad's father, and John's wife sat near them, watching the little boy playing. On the windowsill behind them were some wine-glasses John had set out for sale; suddenly one of the glasses launched itself off the sill and halfway across the room, smashing into pieces in the middle of the train track. The father looked round, asking 'Who threw that?' – a pointless question, because it was obvious to everyone that there was no one else there. Then everyone in the room watched in amazement as another glass lifted itself from the windowsill and flew across the room towards them. Not surprisingly the father grabbed his son by the hand and ran with him out of the shop – and John has never seen him again.

Fortunately such terrifying occurrences were rare – or John might have been forced out of business altogether. There were already several people who wouldn't come into the shop, and several who had been inside once and vowed never to return. Certainly things did seem to calm down a little after this last disturbing episode. In fact, things seemed so peaceful that John began to wonder if the haunting had run its course and ended for ever. It was nice to think this way, but another year passed before John received the confirmation that he and his shop would be left alone for good. The way that confirmation arrived was as spooky as anything that had come before.

One day a lady came into the shop, clearly out of breath, and asked if she could sit down for a while. John offered her a chair, and she sank into it gratefully. Then she began to empty the contents of her handbag onto the table next to her. John watched her with some concern as she scattered her bits and pieces over his valuable table, wondering if she were settling in for a long stay. Eventually she located what she was searching for – brandishing an airmail letter, she asked John if she could read the letter to him. By this time John had decided that she was definitely a bit odd and it was probably best to humour her, so he agreed to listen.

Before she began, she asked John if he had heard or seen anything strange in the shop. John guardedly told her about the rapping noises, and a couple of the other odd incidents. The woman smiled a reassuring smile. 'Not to worry,' she told him, 'it's only Grandma.' She then told him that she had lived in Churchtown all her life, and her Grandmother, Emma May Bailey, had once run the sweet shop in this very building.

Then she began to read the letter. It was from her brother, who had emigrated to Australia many years before. He had written to his sister to relate a strange dream, in which he had seen his Grandmother Bailey. She had told him to go to Little Thatch Antiques and tell Mr and Mrs Jebb that she was quite happy to leave her shop in their care. As he had not been back to Churchtown in decades and did not recognise the name of the shop, let alone the name Jebb, he had asked his sister and asked her to check these details, and if possible, pass the message on. This was, by anybody's standards, astonishing news. But the final evidence was yet to come.

A while later another local woman came to visit John. She had been in his shop only once before – she had popped in to have a look around and almost immediately said she would have to leave again – she had felt a presence in the shop so strongly that she broke out into goose-pimples and wasn't at all happy with the sensation. John found himself telling the woman that she might be right about a 'presence', and he told her everything that had happened up until then, including his friend's previous description of a little old woman in a black dress.

When this local lady came to visit again, she refused to come into the shop, but asked John to come to the door and look at a photograph she had found. It turned out that she was very interested in local history, and after hearing his story had gone away and done some research into the background of the building. Finally she had come across the photograph of a little old lady who had owned the building at the turn of the century, when it had been a sweet shop. The lady was wearing a bonnet, and a long black dress with a pinafore, and she was not more than five feet tall. Her name? Emma May Bailey . . .

Since then, John has been able to run his business quietly, with no more unwelcome intrusions from ghostly hands throwing things about and frightening away his customers. Grandma Bailey obviously approves of him and his wife, and having passed the message on that she would not bother him again, has kept to her word. But that doesn't necessarily mean she has gone forever. At least twice, a little old woman has been seen late at night or in the early hours of the morning, walking along the street in front of the Little Thatch Antique Shop and disappearing – literally – down the side-entry. If Little Thatch Antiques ever changes hands again, she might be back . . .

LYDIA BELL

When the Bell family arrived at their summer residence in Scarborough, in the summer of 1804, they could not have envisaged the tragedy which was to befall them. They had travelled from York, where Mr Bell had a profitable confectionery business. By the standards of the day he was more than comfortably well-off, able to bring his wife and daughter to their holiday mansion on St Nicholas Street for several weeks every year. His daughter Lydia had happy memories of childhood holidays, but she was fast changing from a child into a young woman, no longer happy to spend her days building sand-castles and her evenings quietly in her room. She was a vivacious attractive girl, beginning to become aware of her effect on young men. And during the summer of 1804 Lydia struck up a holiday romance which was to have terrible consequences.

Her beau was a young officer, stationed with the York Volunteers at the Castle Hill barracks in the town. He was a presentable young man, and under normal circumstances Lydia's father might well have approved of him as an escort for his daughter. But unfortunately these were not normal circumstances. There is nothing new about fleeting holiday romances, and Mr Bell felt that his inexperienced daughter's feelings were at risk of being seriously hurt. Scarborough was far enough from York as it was, and who knew anything about this young man? How could Lydia expect anything respectable to come from this liaison? The Bells were a family of some social standing and Lydia's actions were threatening to provoke scandalous gossip.

Refusing to listen to her pleas, Mr Bell sternly forbade her to encourage the young officer's attentions. A terrible argument ensued, which resulted in his taking the radical step of locking poor Lydia in her room every evening, whilst he and his wife went out to seek some entertainment.

Lydia was a headstrong girl, and not about to give in to her father so easily. She managed to talk a neighbour into releasing her from her room occasionally so that she could go walking in the town. One particular night, after enlisting again the help of her neighbour, she went off happily, wearing her favourite pink gown. She was never seen alive again. Lydia Bell's body was found the next morning, at the low water mark on Scarborough's South Sands. She was still wearing her favourite pink dress. She had been cruelly strangled.

The first suspicion immediately fell on the young officer with whom Lydia had been so enamoured, and he was duly charged with her murder. Although he vehemently denied any involvement, four people were willing to swear that they had seen Lydia and the officer together on the evening in question: a young man named Val Nicholson and his three friends, William Short, Jonathan Simpson, and Robert Johnson. Despite their testimonies the prosecution was unable to find any real evidence to prove beyond doubt that the officer was guilty as charged. In the event he was acquitted, and the murderer's identity remained a mystery for many years.

Apart from Lydia's tormented parents, there was one other person present at court for whom the matter could not rest. By all accounts, Val Nicholson led a wandering, restless life after the trial. He suffered from an illness which caused him to suffer fits of delirium, and often during these fits he saw the lovely young Lydia in front of him. He would call to his wife to come and see her, begging her to drive the vision away from him. Finally, on his deathbed, he confessed that it was he who had murdered the girl. He had met her that fateful evening, induced her to follow him along a cliff path and there, with the waves pounding on the rocks far below, a violent argument had ensued which ended in Lydia being strangled and thrown over the edge. His friends had all perjured themselves in court to try and save him, and it had worked . . . as far as court justice went. But his guilty memories had plagued him endlessly until only a deathbed confession released him from a lifetime of guilt. Nicholson's friends had long since died, all, it was rumoured, of untimely deaths . . .

Lydia's ghost, wearing her pink dress, has been seen many times in the Bell family home, and in the immediate vicinity, by different residents of the house. A certain Mrs Agnes Clarke, who had lived there as a child, explained that the top rooms of the house had been converted into a playroom, and as she and her young cousin had played there one day they had both seen a lady in pink move from one side of the room to the other.

A slightly more romantic story is told of an artist who chose to paint a scene featuring the exterior of the fine old house, including the imposing stone steps at the back of the building. When he was asked why he had painted a lady in a pink dress walking up the steps, he explained it was a touch of artistic licence, based on tales his grandfather had told him of often seeing the woman, when he had lived there.

In the late 1940's the Bell's holiday mansion was renovated and reorganised into several self-contained flats with business premises on the ground floor. During this period of intense work a crane-driver was obliged to stay overnight, but he only stayed the once. The next morning he would not speak of what he had experienced, but swore he would never stay there alone again. Then a woman who had grown up in one of the converted flats remembered that when she was a child, a lady in pink had tried to prevent her from entering the house . . .

More recently, a woman living in the house said that she had often heard the rustling sound of a lady in an old-fashioned dress walking up the stairs, and on one occasion she had even seen a woman – wearing a pink dress, of course – resting in a chair.

A few years ago a group of psychics camped out in the old Bell home. Their intention was to contact poor Lydia and convince her that her search was pointless, and the time had come for her to move on. It seems they were successful. As far as we know, the ghost of this particular Lady in a Pink Dress has never been seen again.

THE GHOSTS OF MALLERSTANG

Mallerstang Dale on the borders of Westmorland is an almost forgotten valley that must still look much as it did when Viking settlers named it, over a thousand years ago. The River Eden winds along its limestone bed in the valley bottom, shaded by the occasional crippled oak or rowan. To either side the fells soar upwards, dotted with sheep on the lower flanks and sheering off into crags where peregrine falcons still survive. One of the loneliest stretches of railways still in use, the Settle to Carlisle line, runs along its length over viaducts fantastically engineered by navvies a hundred and fifty years ago. The drystone farms and houses strung out in the valley are few, mostly hundreds of years old, and are themselves built on older sites of habitation.

It is not only the silence and isolation of this austerely beautiful valley that haunts the memory of all who have experienced it. The historic events that have shaped the country outside Mallerstang have left their ghostly traces behind, and there is scarcely a house or fell without its own strange story or unexplained happenings attached to it.

Anne Byrne owns an old farmhouse which she runs as a Bed-and-Breakfast in Shoregill, a little hamlet lying between the Eden River and the railway higher up the fellside. She and all her family learned to live with a ghost which made itself at home after her daughter was born. One evening shortly after the birth, her son was watching television when he heard the door latch rattle behind him, opening and closing the door. Thinking it was his brother he turned around, but there stood another lad, dressed in a flat cap, braces and knickerbockers, who walked through the room, through the wall, and disappeared.

The Ribblehead viaduct on route of the Settle to Carlisle railway, which runs through Mallerstang valley.

In the months that followed, her sons often saw the old-fashioned boy, although the figure Anne has seen has had its face shrouded in black. Then one day through the baby intercom, she heard her daughter babbling happily, and a second voice answering her. Anne knew there was nobody else in the house, but rushed upstairs just to make sure. The baby's room, normally so cosy, was suddenly like stepping into a fridge. Needless to say, there was nobody else but the baby there.

When even her guests even started remarking on the curiously dressed young boy they had glimpsed around the house, Anne decided to consult a medium, even though the family did not feel intimidated in any way by these strange appearances. After the medium had been in the house for a few hours, she told Anne that the boy meant no harm, but was acting as a sort of a 'guardian angel' to the baby, and would go when he felt he was no longer needed. He seemed to feel that this was his duty because he had lived in this house before, in the time when the railway was being built at Shoregill.

The medium had experienced a similar 'guardianship' of a child in the area, where a toddler had often babbled about 'a lady' in her room. One afternoon, the child was discovered toppled on her back and crying at the head of a steep flight of stairs. Not having many words, the little girl could only repeat 'The lady pushed me over!' The family and the medium concluded that 'The Lady', whoever she was, had prevented the child from falling forwards down the stairs by pushing her backwards. Once a stairgate was fitted, they heard no more about The Lady. Sure enough, when Anne Byrne's daughter grew out of toddlerhood, the knickerbocker boy appeared less and less . . . and he has not been seen now for several years.

There have been many other strange events in Mallerstang, and some seem to continue to this day. The oldest legend is told about the dramatic sight that looms above the traveller coming upon the valley from its northern end, where the massive outline of Wild Baugh Fell can be seen, most often against a lowering sky. It is a skyline that has sent one man, in particular, almost out of his mind . . .

In 1170, the people of England had been horrified by the murder of Thomas à Becket, the Henry II's archbishop, in Canterbury Cathedral. One of the four knights who had assisted at the murder by guarding the massive doors of the cathedral was Sir Hugh de Morville. After the deed was done he fled to the remote northern hills to try and evade the wrath of the people, and found himself in hiding in Mallerstang. But across the valley from where he was hiding he was confronted by the outline of Wild Baugh Fell. In the menacing stillness of the valley, silent but for the sound of the wind, the fell seemed to him to take on the profile he remembered of the murdered archbishop, still wearing his mitre, as he lay on his back on the altar steps . . . Day after day, the sight tortured his conscience, and he knew he could never rest until he had atoned for his crime. Nobody found Sir Hugh's hiding-place in Mallerstang, and he eventually escaped to France where, it is said, he led a saintly life in an obscure monastery until he died. But some say that Sir Hugh's spirit has never left Mallerstang. The fellside where he hid became known as 'Hugh's Seat', and on some wild nights a light has been seen way up where there is no habitation, flickering from Hugh's Seat across the valley to Wild Baugh Fell.

Many locals swear that unexplained flickering lights are also seen further down the valley at Boggle Green, and that is a place to be avoided. A Boggle is a northern word of Norse origin meaning a black creature, or witch, of malign intent. No local will walk past Boggle Green after sundown. One possible attempt to control what evil lurks at Boggle Green was recently found during renovations at Deepgill Farm, which lies close by. As builders were altering the fireplace, three clouded glass bottles full of bent pins were found under the hearth. Unthinkingly, the builder threw them in the skip – and from then on, there was no peace while Deepgill was being renovated. Doors rattled and slammed, tools went missing, and crashes and bangs reverberated, lights switched themselves on and off through the empty ancient farmhouse. After some research, the owner discovered that the bottles of bent pins must have been placed there when the house was built, as an ancient remedy against the effects of witchcraft and evil spirits. The bottles were retrieved from the skip and carefully put back, since when peace has returned to Deepgill.

The land owned by Deepgill Farm extends to The Thrang – a grey stone, early Victorian house by the roadside, now converted into a cosy little hotel. Its turrets and gables rise among the firs and cedars around it and it commands views of the lonely valley road and the fells

rising before and behind it. 'Thrang" is an old Norse word for a busy meeting place of people, and the house is thought to derive its name from the bridge crossing the Eden next to the house, where the drovers' road dips down at last from the hill tops to Boggle Green and the river. It is also thought that this crossroads was once the site of a gibbet, where the regular sight of a criminal's corpse creaking and twisting in the Mallerstang gales would modify any lawless inclinations of the locals. It is known that in 1537 ten local men were hanged in the valley for taking part in the Pilgrimage of Grace, after begging in vain to Henry VIII for alms and mercy after his desecration of the monasteries.

Possibly because of its proximity to Thrang Bridge, Boggle Green and Deepgill, The Thrang has rarely been quiet, even when an empty ruin. When Wyn Hamilton and her husband first saw the ruined house

The Thrang Hotel in Mallerstang Valley, with Wild Baugh Fell and Deepgill Farm in the background.

and decided to renovate it into a home and hotel, the locals muttered discouragements. 'The Thrang? Its haunted', they were bluntly told. No one liked to pass by at night. There were tales of lights in the sightless ruined windows, and a cold atmosphere . . . One old lady offered a more cheerful perspective – were they psychic and if so, would the voices of the two old ladies at The Thrang bother the Hamiltons, she asked? When, rather startled, the Hamiltons replied that they didn't think so, she said, 'That's good. If you love the Thrang, you'll see them. But there's nothing there that will harm you . . . '

The Hamiltons had moved into the area ten years previously but were still regarded as 'offcomers' or strangers. Accordingly, they scoffed at such tales, and soon the old house had new owners and was filled from attic to cellar with builders.

In the cellar of The Thrang the builders discovered a deep well which had been sealed up. The Hamiltons were delighted, as the house was not linked to any water mains. Here was a pure water supply to back up the storage tank outside on the fell. But once again the locals warned them about a local superstition that wells, once capped, should never be uncapped again, for fear of evils that might be released as a result. But the Hamiltons had had enough of this sort of advice, and asked Jerry, their builder, to unseal the well while they went back to London. He set to work and eventually cleared the well out. But as he peered into its depths he felt a tremendous thwack on the back of his head which nearly sent him toppling over into it. He straightened up in terror and looked behind him – but there was no one there.

From that moment on there was hardly a quiet moment in the house, and the more the house was knocked about and repaired, the greater the answering 'protest' seemed to be. Apart from the usual complaints of tools vanishing and re-appearing, Jerry swore that unlocked doors would lock, or locked doors swing open. Boxes and chairs were thrown around rooms they knew to be empty. Two pairs of footsteps, one old and slow, the other brisker, could be heard beginning half-way up the stairs, and continuing along the passage. It got to the stage where Jerry barricaded the door against the nocturnal commotion which, surprisingly, subsided for a few days when he at last yelled out a few choice expletives to quell the row.

By now Jerry was seriously rattled and asked a friend, Philip, to come and help with the building work and keep him company in the evenings. He explained what had happened, although Philip didn't really know what to make of his excited catalogue of events. But that week something was to happen which would change Philip's mind as well.

One morning, thinking himself alone in the house, Philip was having a bath in a newly renovated bathroom which did not yet have its door attached. All of a sudden he froze in astonishment. Just outside the doorway he could clearly hear whispering voices, although he couldn't quite make out what was being said. It was a still day, there was no wind outside. The voices continued. Philip leapt out of the bath and poked his head around the corner – but there was no one there. He rushed out into the garden and sat there, dressed only in a towel, waiting for Mrs Hamilton to return from her shopping. Nothing in the world would induce him to return into the house alone.

Mrs Hamilton didn't know what to make of these tales. Neither she, nor her husband, nor their two dogs, seemed to sense anything amiss. However, it was true that she was finding it increasingly hard to keep a workforce at The Thrang. Then, a couple of months later, she lost her electricians as well . . .

The two local lads, Tony and Frank, were working late in the attic room, wiring out the top floor. They had already become a little unsettled by the fact that their tools seemed to keep vanishing, and them appearing again at opposite ends of the room to where they had been working. But it is easy to disregard these things which seem to happen to everyone. They were packing up in the early hours and Tony went downstairs to put the toolbox in the car.

Suddenly he felt the back of his neck prickle. Turning around, he saw a grey figure in the passage behind him. He bolted down to the carpark, opened the boot and flung in the toolbox, yelling to Frank to come and get in the car. Frank looked out of the attic window to see what the commotion was all about – and was sure he saw a figure standing behind Tony. He in his turn then rushed downstairs, out of the door which he left unlocked in his haste, past the open boot and dived into the front seat next to Tony. 'Let's get out!' he gasped. The car did a skidding two-point turn out of the little car park, and as they shot away Frank looked back up at the attic window and was sure he saw another grey figure there, willing them to go. It wasn't until they got a couple of miles down the road to the hamlet of Outhgill that they even stopped to close the car boot.

As these accounts of strange happenings at the Thrang began to pile up, Wyn Hamilton began to research the history of the house. It had apparently been built on the site of two much older cottages built in the 1680's. In 1830 the Reverend John Fawcett combined and extended the cottages into a vicarage, where he lived with his five daughters – only one of whom married and left the valley. The other four spent their whole lives at the Thrang. From old plans it is clear that a passage and stairway originally began half-way up the present staircase. A hundred years later an historian of the area, John Grey, then bought the house, and lived there for many years with his mother and sister. Although he moved away to Cambridge, his mother and sister remained in the house until they died.

The disturbances seemed to diminish as the renovations came to a close, but for some extra comfort Mrs Hamilton, who had been brought up as a Catholic, asked a friend who was a priest to bless the house and say a Mass in the now beautiful drawing room. At last there seemed to be peace.

In the last year or so the Hamiltons have began to make plans for their retirement, which might possibly involve selling part or all of the house and its outbuildings which they have come to love. Recently a guest reading in the hall parlour barely raised her head from her book to greet Rosemary, the only other lady guest she knew was in the house, who came and sat down opposite her before the dinner gong was struck. A few seconds later the gong did ring out – and as she got up she saw the chair opposite was empty. Then Rosemary herself came down the stairs for dinner, and assured her friend that she had not sat in that chair all evening. Since then a quiet sobbing has been heard about the house, which was tracked down to an empty room at the end of the passage where the electricians saw the grey figure. Was it the cat? Or have the guardians of the house, whoever they are, sensed and lamented the changes in the air?

WILLINGTON MILL

Edmund Procter had spent his early childhood in a haunted house . . . or so it seemed.

The house stood near a corn mill at Willington, Wallsend, close to the Newcastle and Shields Railway. Edmund had always harboured strange memories of the place. He had been born there, and during his life there were many occasions when he would recall things that had happened in the house when he was a child – things that seemed to have no natural explanation. He and his family – God-fearing Quakers all – had left the Mill House and moved to North Shields when he was only seven. As he grew up he reasoned that his weird memories were probably the result of his childish imagination having run riot. It wasn't until his father, Joseph, died in 1875 that Edmund found the proof he had been looking for. Amongst his father's belongings he found a diary, written during the years at Willington, which described *in great detail* events which Edmund only half-remembered. It proved to him that he had been right all along. He *had* spent his early childhood in a haunted house.

Joseph began his diary in 1835. He gave as his reason for writing the fact that his wife was concerned about the family's nursemaid who had recently confessed that for the past three months she had been frightened by the sounds of strangely heavy footsteps coming from the room above the nursery where she looked after the children. She knew full well that the room was uninhabited, and yet she could not ignore the footsteps – which were so real and so heavy-footed that they made the very windows rattle in their frames.

The family were sympathetic. They searched the upper floor for signs of an intruder – but found nothing. Within days, every family member had also heard the strange noises coming from the room above the nursery. The nursemaid was so disturbed that she resigned her post and another maid was taken on in her place. The new girl was told nothing about the noises, but after a short time she too began to hear someone moving around upstairs, sweeping the floor, laying a fire, when she *knew* that no one was up there.

The noises were not confined to the evening hours: they happened at any hour of the day or night. Edmund's mother was in the nursery one morning when she heard the distinct sound of a man's heavy shoes waking towards the window and back again. That same day at dinner, the maid who had been with the children in the nursery came downstairs to check that Joseph was dining and was not walking about upstairs to frighten her.

The room above the nursery had not been used for many years. There was no access to the room from outside, as the window was boarded up and even the door was nailed. The chimney was inaccessible, and the fireplace was covered by a fireguard which was so covered in soot and dust that any movement would be immediately obvious. Every possible natural explanation was considered – even the chance that the room might be infested with enormous rats. Though the largest imaginable rat could not make the floor vibrate with its footsteps . . .

Joseph noted in his diary that after some months the footsteps had stopped. Other manifestations had taken their place. Whilst soothing their youngest child to sleep in the evening, both Joseph and his wife distinctly heard taps on the leg of the wooden cradle and felt the vibration of the taps – as if they had been made by a piece of metal. A respectable neighbour reported having seen a transparent white female figure in the window of the room on the second storey of the house. A while later, Thomas Mann, the foreman of the flour mill, who lived his own house next door, was summoned by his wife to witness a similar luminous transparent apparition in the window. It looked like a priest in a white surplice. Joseph's sister-in-law was lodging with the Manns at the time. She and the rest of the family were also summoned to see the apparition, which remained full ten minutes before disappearing – by fading away from the head downwards. The room in which she (or it) appeared was Joseph's own room.

Joseph's diary continues with comments about several small events which happened over a long period. His wife felt her bed being lifted into the air and than let down again. One of the children came crying that the same thing had happened to his crib. Footsteps were heard. Closet doors slammed shut. The children were scared one evening by a loud clattering sound coming from a cupboard. Bumps and thuds were often heard from unoccupied rooms above.

The diary had begun in 1835. By 1840 the haunting had developed from the original footsteps to a whole catalogue of phenomena. Various family members heard voices around them. Sometimes these were completely unintelligible. Sometimes the words were audible but conveyed no meaning – such as 'come and get' or 'never mind'. The children were becoming frightened of going into their bedrooms during the day – never mind at night – for fear of hearing a voice or some other fearful sound.

In July 1840 a certain Dr. Drury heard about the occurrences at Willington Mill and sought permission to bring a friend and stay awake in the house all night in the hope of witnessing the events for himself. He got more than he bargained for. About one in the morning Joseph heard a shriek, hurried to the stairs, and found Dr. Drury lying on the floor in a dead faint. He had seen the ghost. It had walked across the room towards him on the landing. He had seen it with perfect clarity. So clearly had he seen it, and so frightening had he found it, that it had caused the doctor to pass out cold with shock.

Dr Drury described his experience in a letter at a friend. This is his own account of what happened:

I took out my watch to ascertain the time, and found that it wanted ten minutes to one. In taking my eyes from the watch, they became riveted upon a closet door, which I distinctly saw to open, and saw also the figure of a female attired in greyish garments, with the head inclining downwards, and one hand pressed upon the chest, as if in pain, and the other viz. the right hand, extended towards the floor, with the index finger pointed downwards. It advanced with an apparently cautious step across the floor towards me; immediately as it approached my friend, who was slumbering, its right hand was extended towards him; I then rushed at it, giving at the time . . . a most awful yell; but instead of grasping it, I fell upon my friend, and I recollect nothing distinctly for nearly three hours afterwards. I have since learnt that I was carried downstairs in an agony of fear and terror.

At the end of December 1840, after fourteen months of almost constant activity, the haunting stopped. All was quiet for almost five months. But in May 1841 Joseph's wife noticed that the staff were a little edgy. She questioned them and found they had been experiencing the ghosts again – but had not wanted to say anything. She had been ill and they had not wanted to worry her. In the ensuing months there were the usual bumps and bangs and heavy footsteps. The children began to complain of hearing someone call their names. In November of that year, Joseph went into the children's room and found all the children searching beneath the bed for a 'monkey' which they had all seen quite clearly, but which had disappeared under the bed. It wasn't there now, but the children's insistence convinced Joseph that they had been telling the truth.

Despite the doctor's investigation, there was no change in the level of activity at the Mill. The awful visitations continued to haunt the family and their visitors for years. In 1847 the household moved to North Shields. There were many reasons for their move, but doubtless they felt it would be a good thing to take their children away from the Mill House. The family's last night in the house was one of the busiest ever, with the sounds of boxes being dragged downstairs, footsteps stamping about the place, doors slamming, furniture being shifted – as if the ghosts themselves were preparing to move house. Thankfully the haunting did *not* follow the family, and their life in their new home was entirely free from the nerve-shattering events they had endured for almost ten years at Willington.

Not only an exciting story in itself, this type of case is always of interest to researchers, for it has two useful features. First there is the testimony of people who are used to describing things in detail. In this case there is Dr. Drury. His letter, quoted above, gives us a rare insight into what it is like to make contact with a ghost. After reading his account it is amazing how close his experiences were with those fictional versions where the would-be investigator, when confronted by the spectre, shouts 'Get it!' and runs towards the apparition – only to run away again in complete panic.

The second useful feature is that there is further information about the occupants who stayed in the Mill before and after the family whose story we have heard. Apparently Joseph's cousins had stayed in the mill for some twenty-five years before the events described above. Although they had heard that the place was haunted, they had no strange experiences. Some of those who stayed at the place after Joseph had left *did* have strange experiences, but the haunting was by no means as extreme as it was during Joseph's tenancy.

What was the cause of the strange phenomena at Willington Mill House? The building was only thirty years old when the haunting began. Although there were rumours that the builder's mother-in-law had lived and died there, no evidence was found to support the idea that her spirit could be the cause of such a wide variety of events. The house no longer exists but over .the years various researchers have tested their theories and followed up leads – all to no avail.

The one thing we can be sure of is that the account of the haunting of Willington Mill was not deliberately mendacious. Joseph, as we have seen, was respected as God-fearing. Edmund was in all respects his father's son. In 1892 Edmund submitted his father's diary to the Society of Psychical Research, accompanied by his own notes and recollections of his childhood at Willington. Whilst he can offer no explanation of what occurred there, we cannot but believe that every word contained in those notes was, to the writer, the absolute truth. 'I am merely recording facts as simply as I can', he wrote, 'readers may smile or mock as seemeth good unto them. I cannot alter what has taken place to suit them or anyone else.'

SAMLESBURY OLD HALL

During the Lancashire cotton riots in 1878, a young sub-altern was garrisoned with his company at Samlesbury Hall, near Blackburn. In the early morning he was awakened by the sound of a woman crying bitterly in the corridor outside his room. He got out of bed to investigate but could find no one; the next morning he mentioned this to his host and hostess, and saw the look they passed between them. He had witnessed the White Lady of Samlesbury Hall. In 1926, when he was an elderly Colonel, he wrote to the London Morning Post and told them the whole story.

In view of the years that had passed, the Colonel may have misremembered the details when he wrote his letter to the papers, but he certainly experienced something that morning which he was never able to satisfactorily explain.

In 1960, the papers were again full of reports of strange happenings at Samlesbury Hall; or more accurately, on the road close by. Several motorists had reported seeing a woman dressed in white at the roadside – some stopped to offer her assistance or a lift, particularly if the weather was bad, and others saw her walk into the road and were sure they had hit and killed her, but all of them were shocked when they realised that *she wasn't really there.*

Although the staff at Samlesbury Hall claim never to have seen the White Lady and are sceptical of her existence, there is no doubt that other people, who have no expectation of seeing any kind of ghost in the area, certainly do see something. The White Lady has been seen on the road, in the gardens, and in the Hall itself. There is a theory that such ghosts appear less frequently as the years pass, before fading away entirely, but as recently as 1987, a motorist travelling with his wife along this busy road at night, not only saw the White Lady too late to avoid hitting her, but actually felt his car bump over something solid. He stopped, got out, and searched everywhere but had to admit there was no 'body'. Even pedestrians have reported seeing her standing at the roadside, and are mystified when she simply disappears.

But who is the White Lady? The young sub-altern in 1878, when questioning his host and hostess about the mysterious weeping he had heard that night, was given the traditional explanation:

In the latter half of the sixteenth century, Lancashire was a stronghold for the Catholic faith, at a time in Britain's history when such loyalty was often rewarded with death. Samlesbury Hall was the seat of the Southworth family, who were intensely loyal Catholics. Like many of the landed Lancashire families at the time, they risked their lives by providing a secret sanctuary – in this case a Priest Room – for Catholic priests hiding from the authorities who were determined to rid the area of all traces of 'popery'. Catholic religion. Sir John Southworth was known to support Mary Queen of Scots and wished to see her reinstated on the throne, and his nephew John was ordained as a priest, and canonised in 1970 as the last Catholic to die for his faith in England. His son Christopher was an equally devout and strong defender of their faith, and it is he who is the villain of this piece, for unfortunately Christopher's love of his religion caused him to turn against his two of his own family members: Jane, and Dorothy. He conspired for Jane to be tried as a witch – and he also murdered Dorothy's Protestant lover.

Jane came to be tried as a witch in 1612 because she began to show signs of taking up the Protestant faith. In all, nine Samlesbury people were accused of witchcraft, three of whom, Jane Southworth and Janet and Ellen Bierley, were taken to Lancaster to be tried. The case was regarded as so important that significantly it was tried in the same assize session as the infamous Pendle witch trial.

The main witness was a simple girl of 14, Grace Sowerbutts of Samlesbury, the granddaughter of Janet Bierley, and the niece of Ellen. Grace accused all three women of bewitching her so that she began to waste away, and she said that her grandmother Janet had turned herself into a black dog which had walked on its hind legs and tried to talk Grace into drowning herself. All three women were accused of taking Grace to a twice-weekly Sabbath on the banks of the River Ribble where they were joined in their demonic parties by 'four black things, going upright, and yet not like men in the face . . . '

Fortunately, even though witchcraft trials were regularly hearing such fabrications and sentencing the accused to death, the judge found Grace's statements hard to believe, and chose to cross-examine her. Under pressure, she admitted that she had been persuaded to denounce the women by Christopher Southworth. Jane and the others were acquitted, and Christopher's cruel plot against his own sister-in-law was foiled. It is highly likely that Jane had embraced the Church of England and that this was the reason for Christopher's victimisation of her.

Cruel as this was, Christopher's treatment of his sister Dorothy was to prove even more tragic. Dorothy fell in love with a young man of the de Hoghton family, from nearby Hoghton Towers; he would have been suitable enough had he not renounced his faith in favour of the Church of England, and on these grounds Dorothy's father strictly forbade the union, and ordered the young man never to come near his daughter again. But true love never will be denied, and Dorothy and her lover continued to meet in secret and eventually planned an elopement.

Unfortunately Christopher became aware of this plan, and at the appointed time he ambushed de Hoghton and his attendant and murdered them outside Dorothy's bedroom window. Dorothy witnessed the awful deed, threw herself from the window and was killed.

The window of the Priest Room at Samlesbury Hall.

This is only one version of the legend, which naturally has changed through the years; another version claims that Dorothy was sent away to a convent on the continent and there went mad with grief and died. The number of people murdered also varies, according to the source consulted; maybe two people were murdered, or maybe three, or perhaps it was only the young de Hoghton. Who can tell?

Looking for the truth of such legends is always fraught with difficulties, but credence was lent to the story in 1826 when a road was being dug near the Hall and two human skeletons were uncovered. But then again, only a few years ago workmen were laying drains and came across yet another skeleton, male, lying against the foundation wall.

Another problem is that the Southworth family pedigree shows that Sir John had no daughter named Dorothy. Perhaps she may have married into the family; she would not therefore have been recorded in the pedigree. Not far away is – or was – Old Pleasington Hall, and a daughter of the family there was called Dorothy, and she is recorded as marrying a Southworth, then a de Hoghton, then Thomas Ainsworth, who was likewise a Protestant. On the other hand, it was not unusual for families to arrange for any member who had transgressed beyond forgiveness to be totally excised from the records . . .

But despite the difficulty of proving exactly who the White Lady is, if you should be driving down the A677 past the beautiful black and white building that is Samlesbury Hall, be aware that if you see a lady dressed in white standing by the roadside, *she isn't really there . . .* particularly if the month is August, for this is the anniversary of her death . . .

Samlesbury Old Hall next to the stretch of road where motorists have claimed to see the White Lady.

THE WEB OF DEATH

Although the names of the characters have been changed, this story is based entirely on a letter received by the authors, soon after an interview on Radio Lancashire. The author of the letter, called Bill Johnson in the story, assures us that the tale is absolutely true.

Bill Johnson and Pete Graham were the very best of friends. From earliest childhood they had lived and played together in the same little back street in Manchester. Their friendship lasted throughout their lives – and perhaps a little longer.

When the second World War began, the two young men joined the army together, and fought in the same Regiment. In many a tight spot, when life and death were in the balance, they relied on each other for comfort and protection. When VE Day at last arrived they celebrated the end of the war with enthusiasm. They had survived – and so had their friendship.

After the war the two friends went back to Manchester. Each met a girl and fell in love. When Bill married, Pete was his Best Man. When Pete's turn came, Bill returned the service of friendship. The years passed. Babies were born. Although Bill and Pete were now busy family men with many duties to perform and many bills to pay, their friendship never faltered.

But then Pete's wife left him and emigrated to Australia – taking their children with her. Bill wondered if his friend would ever recover from the pain. Pete felt that everything he had worked for had been taken from him. He felt he had no reason to go on living, sank into drink. As Bill saw it, his friend drank a little too much, a little too often and was in danger of becoming seriously ill. But still the two men's friendship survived. Many were the conversations they shared over a few pints. They talked about life, what may come after life, and what the point of it all might be. Sometimes they spoke, half-jokingly, about the possibility of being reincarnated in another body, and what they would choose to be 'next time around'.

Then Bill's wife died. Pete tried to be a good friend, but was too confused by his own problems to offer much help. He was still drinking . . . Bill could only sympathise. He could easily have turned to the bottle himself under the weight of his own loss. He was only thankful that he was less fragile than his friend.

Then one day Pete called to tell Bill that he had met a woman with whom he had fallen deeply in love. Bill was delighted for him. His delight was only slightly dampened by the news that Pete was going with his new wife to start a fresh life in another part of the country. Bill did not see Pete again for many years – but he often thought of his old friend. He was sure that Pete was happy with his new life away from the scene of his first disastrous marriage.

Then one night there was a quite knock on Bill's door. He opened it to see a frail, white-haired man, barely supporting himself on two black sticks. It took Bill a few moments to realise that the gaunt figure was his old friend Pete Graham. And any pleasure he felt at this unexpected visit faded as he looked a more closely into Pete's eyes. Fifteen years had passed. But it was something more than the passage of time that showed in Pete's staggering unsteady gait and in his gaunt face. It was obvious to Bill that his friend was desperately ill.

As they sat down to drink a pot of tea, Bill asked Pete what was wrong. 'I haven't long to live,' Pete wheezed. Bill didn't understand all the long words Pete used to describe his various illnesses, but realised his friend was dying. Pete seemed to be resigned to his fate, and strangely content. 'I just wanted to see my old mate once more, before

I die', he whispered.

The visit was short – which was something of a relief to Bill. For though he was very glad to see his old friend, he found it difficult to hide his deep sadness at Pete's terrible illness and did not know what to say. Pete saw that his dear friend was upset, and that made him, in turn, uneasy.

Pete looked down at the floor, and, in a voice that seemed to come from deep within, murmured: 'We'll meet again. I'm sure of that. We *will* meet again'.

This seemed to be more than a passing reference to a wartime song. Bill remembered the evenings when he and Pete had talked about what happens after death, and the possibility of reincarnation, the evenings long ago when they had shared many a laugh deciding who – or *what* – they'd like to be in their future existence.

Bill asked Pete if he remembered those conversations. 'Of course I do,' Pete said. 'And I remember,' he added after a pause, 'how we said that if one of us died he would try to come back, *somehow.*'

The two men talked a little longer. Pete reached slowly for his sticks. It was time for him to go. The two friends shook hands with great fondness, promising not to drift apart now they had rediscovered the strength of their fellowship. But they were not to meet again in this life. Less than a month later, Pete Graham died.

A few weeks passed. One winter's evening, after tea, Bill settled in his comfortable armchair to watch television. He did not close the curtains because it was pleasant to look out every now and then. A full moon lit the beautiful, still evening. As he half-watched the news, he suddenly noticed a big, black something among the grey shadows on the wall – something that seemed to be moving towards him.

With a shiver of disgust he realised the dark moving thing was a very large, very black spider.

Bill had a strong aversion to all creeping things. Spiders were the worst of all. He loathed and detested them. He picked up a newspaper, rolled it up and struck out. A second later the spider was dead and knocked onto the floor.

But then, as he settled back into his chair, Bill's eye was caught by something else. Between the television and the dresser was an extraordinarily large and marvellously intricate web. Bill, thinking grimly that the spider wasn't going to need the web any more, rose slowly to his feet to sweep the foul thing away. But as he moved nearer, he noticed that this was no ordinary web. It looked as though the spider had been drunk when he had woven it. The pattern was far from regular. There were the usual radial spokes of silk, but the spaces between them were woven erratically. It looked almost as if the spider had been trying to sign his handiwork with his initials. Bill looked closely, unwilling to believe his eyes.

He could see *two letters* in the web.

The letters were all too clear – a *'P' and a 'G'* – the initials of Pete Graham, his lifelong friend . . .

CHINGLE HALL

...ight in a haunted house, then Goosnargh's
... prior arrangement you can camp out in the
...Room, and try to stay awake all night in the
...or hearing ghostly footsteps. There's certainly
...to set fertile imaginations alight.

...was built by Adam de Singleton in 1260, and
...three..., like many Northern Halls, it became a hide-
out for Catholic priests escaping persecution during the Reformation of
Queen Elizabeth 1 and James 1. It boasts many secret passages and
priest-holes in the walls and floor. Priest-holes are cramped hiding-
places just large enough for a man to have crawled into when the
King's men came on one of their regular raids. They were designed by
specialists, and were often most ingeniously hidden behind chimneys,
rafters or the panelling between two larger rooms. Sometimes they
even existed behind fake 'priest holes' which were designed to be
found quite easily.

As with many ancient buildings, Chingle Hall has many legends
attached to it, such as the one which claims it was the birthplace of St.
John Wall, and that a relic from his body was buried somewhere within
the house. This legend has been researched by the Hall's present
owner, Professor Kirkham, who has found that it cannot be proved or
disproved . . . but this has not harmed the Hall's reputation as one of
the most haunted houses in the country. Many of the hopeful ghost
hunters who stay here emerge entirely unscathed in the morning, but
others have very unsettling stories to tell.

In 1980, when Chingle Hall was still a private residence, a group
of three young men were perhaps the first people to stay overnight as

ghost-watchers, intending to raise money for a charity venture. The evening started quietly enough, but by midnight they had all fled the building. What follows is the story of what happened that night as remembered by Phil, one of the young men.

The window of the Priest's Room at Chingle Hall where Phil spent his terrifying night.

Phil, Alan and Martin, all in their early twenties, ran a thriving mobile disco business they called the 'Route 66 Roadshow'. Three nights a week they entertained at the Blackpool Nurses' Social Club, and with Christmas approaching it seemed a good idea to organise some sort of venture to raise money for a new heart monitor for the Hospital. It was Alan who suggested staying overnight at Chingle Hall, as he was fascinated by ghosts. He had dragged Phil round the place on a couple of occasions, and was tremendously excited by the prospect of staying there. Phil and Martin went along with the idea, for although it seemed a silly way to spend an evening, they could certainly raise a fair amount of money.

It was about seven o'clock on a dark November evening when the lads arrived at the Great Hall, and were shown around the place by the resident owners. The room now called the Great Hall was their lounge, and was well-furnished with a comfortable three piece suite, tables, and a television. The lads were staying in the room above the Hall, which, by contrast, was bare and uncarpeted. The only furniture in the room was a deckchair and a very old desk in the corner. The desk was placed so as to hide a fairly large hole in the wall which led to a priest-hide. As the heater was also in that corner, Phil staked his claim there immediately and Alan and Martin sat on the floor across the room. Alan enthusiastically began setting up his tape-recorder, determined to make sure that if something dramatic happened, he would be fully prepared to record it for posterity.

The minutes and hours passed slowly – there was nothing much to look at in the room, and nothing much to talk about. By ten o'clock, boredom was beginning to set in. They had been there for three hours, but nothing at all spooky had happened. But then they thought that if anything was going to happen, in the best tradition of hauntings it probably wouldn't be until after midnight. Phil, who was sitting in the deckchair by the heater, began to get warm and sleepy, and decided it might be a good idea to doze off for a while, so that later he could wake up and stay awake until the early hours. He laid his head on the desk beside him, using his arm for a cushion, and closed his eyes.

A few minutes later he was violently woken by a very loud bang which came from the desk itself – it had jumped a few inches off the floor and crashed back down again. Phil quickly leapt out of his chair in alarm and looked over his shoulder. He expected to see one of the others standing right behind him, having banged their fist on the desk to frighten him awake. But both his friends were still sitting on the other side of the room, their eyes wide open. Martin was visibly frightened, but Alan was eagerly waiting to see what would happen next. For a few moments all of them sat there in silence, and then Phil decided he'd had enough – it was time to go home!

Alan and Martin managed to talk him out of leaving. They were very excited by what had happened and pointed out to him that it was still only half-past ten. Phil agreed to stay, very grudgingly, as the atmosphere in the room suddenly seemed peculiarly unfriendly. About twenty minutes passed quietly, and even Phil was beginning to relax again, when suddenly there was another bang, this time on the door to the room, a hefty thump which made it sound as though someone obviously wanted to come in! But the owners of the place were still downstairs – the lads could hear 'Starsky and Hutch' on the TV, and in this resonant building with its quota of creaky floorboards they would have heard anyone walking up the stairs.

Alan leapt for the tape-recorder and switched it on, just in time to catch the sound of another loud bang on the door. Even in the dim light Alan's face showed how thrilled he was by this, but Phil stayed exactly where he was, with his back against the wall, frozen to the spot with fear. Then Alan boldly called out: 'If there's anybody there, come in!' The door didn't open, but it seemed as if someone had indeed entered the room, as the uncarpeted wooden floor reverberated with heavy footsteps. Clump, clump, clump, clump, clump, clump. Half a dozen steps came straight towards Phil, who was sitting motionless in his corner in front of the priest-hide. The three of them could feel the floor moving with every step, and for a moment Phil wondered if the people downstairs were playing some stupid trick on them. But if they'd been banging on their ceiling with a broom handle or something of the kind, the floor would have moved *upwards* with each 'step', and that wasn't the case here; the floor was quite definitely being depressed *downwards.*

Alan was absolutely ecstatic, but Phil was petrified and his hair was standing on end. Whatever it was, it was so close to him now that if he'd had the courage he could have reached out his hand and touched it. He didn't, of course, but felt that he could have done . . . Then it began to move again, clump, clump, clump, moving to Phil's left, stopping again in the corner of the room. Alan didn't seem to be able to sense where it was, but Phil was sure of its position, and pointed urgently, 'It's there! It's there!'

After a few seconds they heard it begin to move again, the footsteps sounding like someone wearing heavy boots, moving to the third corner of the room before stopping. They waited for it to move again, thinking it would walk back across the room to the doorway, and go out the same way it had apparently come in. Nothing stirred. A few seconds passed, and then Phil felt the atmosphere lift, and return to normal. He knew that whatever had just happened, it was all over now.

That was enough for Phil. He wasn't listening to any more arguments from his mates, they had come in his car, and he was off home immediately. If they wanted to stay, as far as he was concerned, they could find their own way home in the morning. They had no choice really . . .

Phil still remembers driving away from Chingle Hall that night, and the way he was constantly looking in his rear view mirror until the place was far behind him. And he's not afraid to admit that when the three of them arrived at his home, he talked the others into staying the night to keep him company. They all settled down in the same bedroom, but sleep was out of the question. Alan was still far too excited by what had happened, and he wanted them all to listen to the tape-recording he had made. Phil agreed; he was beginning to wonder if they'd just imagined what had happened. It all seemed too unbelievable.

Alan pressed the 'Play' button. The first bang on the door wasn't there because Alan hadn't pressed the 'Record' button until immediately after that. But the second bang definitely was there. And then they heard Alan's voice, excitedly inviting whoever it was to come into the room. Then, as the footsteps came into the room, another sound came from the tape – a weird sound, as if some unearthly wind was whistling and moaning through the room . . .

LES'S STORY

It was a glorious spring day, with the kind of unexpected warmth that brings the promise of a long hot summer to come and cheers the hearts of ice-cream salesmen, but Les Bond had all but missed it. He had returned home in the early morning after his night-shift at Nelson Fire Station and would have loved to be able to spend the day having a lazy lunch at the pub, or maybe walking through the park, but it just wasn't possible. Duty called – he had no choice but to go to bed and sleep, in preparation for the next night's work.

It was late afternoon when he woke up, disturbed by the sound of someone launching a surprise attack on their lawn with a mower. He lay still for a few minutes, hoping the noise would stop . . . but it didn't. Never mind, it was time he was up anyway.

He left home as usual at five o'clock and set off on the route he always took to the fire station, some miles away. The wonderful weather had put a smile on his face, and he was fully prepared to cope with the rush hour traffic jams and bad tempers. However, he was pleased to find that the traffic was unusually light and there were few other vehicles on the road. Even the A678, the main Blackburn to Burnley road, was unusually quiet – the football season was still in full swing, but it seemed Burnley must have been playing away that evening.

Relaxing into the journey, he turned onto the A6068, a road which would take him from Simonstone to Barrowford, knowing that if there was to be any hold-up it would be on the long S-bend hill which bypasses Higham Village – but to his surprise there were no problems and he was able to speed up the hill at 50 miles an hour. Brilliant! He usually had to crawl up this hill behind labouring lorries, breathing in their foul fumes, and this trouble-free journey was an unexpected treat. Added to that was the beauty of the view from the top of the hill; all that rolling countryside surrounding Burnley and Nelson. The only thing to mar the picture was the smoke from a dozen or more grass fires, which gave a good hint as to how Les and the rest of his shift would be spending their evening. Amazing how a spot of warm weather brought out the carelessness in people . . .

As he was approaching the junction with Higham Hall Road, out of habit he checked his rear-view mirror. There was nothing coming up behind him, and no cars coming towards him – it was safe to maintain his speed, and he did so. The next junction was about half a mile away, where the main road met the road coming from Sabden Fold. Again Les checked his mirror, and this time, to his surprise, he saw a car close behind him, travelling at a similar speed. He did a rapid double-take – where could it have come from? There were no sideroads on this stretch of road, and only a few moments before, there had been nothing behind him at all! The idiot must have travelling at the speed of light to have caught up to him so fast.

Fully alert now, Les was more than a little worried by how close the car was. The driver seemed to be in a terrible hurry, and it looked suspiciously as if he was about to overtake. Les knew they were coming to a place where the road bent in a wide arc, and it was a notoriously dangerous place for such a manoeuvre. The driver must be a stranger to the area, or else he was downright stupid. He watched the car through his rear-view mirror with concern, and was relieved when at last it dropped its speed and widened the gap between them. He realised he had been holding his breath, and let it out with a sigh as he saw that the driver had sensibly decided not to risk overtaking just yet. Or had he? With a stab of horror Les suddenly noticed that the indicator light was flashing – surely he wasn't going to try to overtake after all?

In the mirror, Les watched the car pull out into the road, and he watched it closely, worried because now they were on the most dangerous part of the road and there was no way of telling what might be coming towards them round the next bend. His job as a fireman had given him plenty of chances to see what risks some drivers were prepared to take with their lives, but this was sheer lunacy. He glanced at the grass verge beside the road, deciding it might make a good enough refuge, should anyone suddenly appear coming from the direction of Barrowford.

They were coming to the end of the bend now, where the road straightens out at the junction with Sabden Fold Road, but Les could still see the car behind pulling out further into the road until it was in that blind spot beyond the limit of the rear-view mirror. Les gently touched his brakes, to give the madman a greater chance of overtaking him swiftly and safely, and as he did so he turned his head to the right to see him pass . . . but there was no car. Les's head snapped backward and forward like a clockwork toy, checking the mirror, the road, the mirror, the road, but there was no car, no driver, no indicator . . . *no car at all.*

Les blinked rapidly in disbelief, checking the mirror and the road beside him again and again, unable to believe what his eyes were telling him. There may have been a car there a moment ago, but there was no car there now. Yet where on earth could it have gone? There was nowhere it could have made a right turn. There were a few gateways into fields, but the gates were all closed. In any case, it had been travelling far too fast to have turned into one of them. There was absolutely nowhere for it to have gone. It was as if the car had just disappeared into thin air.

The situation was impossible. Cars don't just disappear. It was still broad daylight, the evening was clear and sunny, and the car had been so *close* behind him. It definitely wasn't a mirage. He had seen a solid vehicle, solid enough for sunlight to reflect off the chrome and the windows, a car with indicators that had flashed. Les hadn't given the driver much attention, he wasn't even sure if it had been a man or a woman . . . then a chilling thought occurred to him – did the car even have a driver? He realised it was crazy thinking; of course the car had a driver, and there must be some sort of logical explanation for what had just happened. But try as he might, Les couldn't think of one. The only explanation he could come up with was that he had just seen a ghost.

Les was frightened. He had been so absolutely aware of that car for several minutes, watching it so closely, how could it have just disappeared? Had he seen an action-replay of an accident, with the car on its final journey to destruction? And if so, how does something like that happen?

In the years that have passed since that day, Les has asked these questions many times, but neither he nor anyone else can give a suitable explanation. Maybe they are questions which never will be answered. Meanwhile, the memory of his experience on that lovely spring evening stays with him, clear in every detail.

THE FYLDE WITCH

St Anne's church, in the village of Woodplumpton, just outside Preston, dates from the fourteenth century. The interior of this ancient church is fascinating and draws many tourists, but just as many come to stare at a nondescript glacial boulder which lies beside a footpath in the churchyard. The boulder marks the grave of the legendary Fylde Witch, Meg Hilton. Tales about Meg the Witch come from all over the Fylde. She is said to have once lived in a tumble-down cottage at Cuckoo Hall, near Wesham.

One story tells how she was accused of stealing corn from a Singleton miller, although he had never managed to catch her in the act. Night after night he would see her sneaking into the mill, but when he went to look for her there was never a trace. In the morning he would check his stores and find corn missing, yet again. Eventually, one night, the miller caught Meg out. He had seen her go into the mill as usual, and though he'd immediately dashed in there after her, she was nowhere to be seen. Convinced he'd been robbed again, the miller counted his stores, and to his surprise found that he had one sack more than he remembered! He swiftly put two and two together, grabbed a pitchfork, and began to jab at the sacks one by one, until one of them let out a scream and there was Meg standing before him. But he still didn't manage to catch hold of her, because she quickly grabbed a broomstick which was lying nearby, jumped astride it and flew away.

Another folktale tells how the Fylde Witch took a liking to a cottage in Catforth, and wanted to move there. The landlord of this area was one Mr Haydock, who was well-known for his love of hunting – he owned several hounds, and his pride and joy was one black dog which was far faster and more lethal than the rest. Meg the Witch went to see Landlord Haydock and made a wager with him; she would turn herself into a hare and race against his hounds, and if she reached her home unscathed, the cottage in Catforth would be hers. Her only stipulation was that the black hound should not be released.

Landlord Haydock accepted her bet, but let loose the black dog anyway. Fortunately, the hare made it to the door of Meg's cottage just as the dog caught up with it, and the best the dog could do before the hare disappeared inside the house was to nip its heel. Meg had won her bet, and she got her cottage at Catforth, but for many days afterwards, it was noticed that she was walking with a slight limp.

Another story tells of a man who came across Meg Hilton returning from market with a fat white goose waddling ahead of her. As the lane was narrow and the bad-tempered bird wouldn't let the man pass, he kicked it out of the way – and the next minute Meg was shouting at him for breaking her pitcher of milk all over the ground. He looked down, and sure enough, on the ground at his feet lay the pieces of a broken milk-crock, in a puddle of wasted milk – and the goose was nowhere to be seen. Apparently, Meg had found the pitcher too heavy to carry, and had turned it into a goose so it could walk home on it's own!

It seems this was a trick Meg used more than once. Another story tells how a farmer saw her flying over a hedge into his cow-pasture with a jug in her hand, and immediately assumed the old hag was set to steal some milk from his cows. He went to see her off, but she argued that she had no jug; she had only come to graze her white goose. The farmer saw through Meg's trick as he spotted milk dribbling from the goose's beak – he kicked at it, the spell was broken, and the milk-jug lay shattered on the ground as Meg flew away over the hedge.

Harmless stories, so far, and it's easy to see how one tale has transposed into another as the centuries have passed. But some of the tales about Meg are far less pleasant. One of the cruellest tells how a farmer, who was sure Meg had bewitched his cow so that it would no longer give milk, decided to take a traditional course of action against her. Pretending to be friendly to the old woman, he invited her to warm herself at his fire, encouraging her to take the cosiest seat, in the inglenook. Before she arrived he had placed two forks, crossed, on her seat, and left them there all day, and thus a spell was put on the old woman so that once seated, she could not stand up again.

Having trapped her there, the farmer berated her for bewitching his cow and insisted she remove the spell straight away. When she proclaimed her innocence, the farmer built up the fire until she became uncomfortably hot, but still she wouldn't confess – not until the flames were so high that they seared the old woman's skin did she at last relent and agree to remove her spell.

Today, it's easy to regard folktales like these as naive stories with no basis in fact – but a woman called Marjorie Hilton really lived, and died, and according to the Parish Register was buried in St Anne's churchyard on the second of May, in the year 1705. It's likely that she was simply a poor old woman, doing her best to survive by stealing small amounts of corn and the odd jugful of milk. In today's liberal climate she would probably have been accepted as a harmless eccentric who preferred solitude to company, but at the end of the seventeenth century, with rumours of witchcraft prevalent in many parts of Lancashire, attitudes were very different. Strange old women like Mother Hilton were always the cause of much speculation and fear.

Even the story of her death is shrouded in mystery. She had not been seen for several days, and when the villagers went to investigate they found her dead. If her death was an accident, it was a strange one indeed, because poor Meg was found crushed between a barrel and a wall. The stories fail to record whether any human agency was suspected of killing her – the verdict of the locals was probably that it was the Devil's work and no further investigation was necessary.

One obvious question is why should a witch be buried in a churchyard? The answer is that while some villagers objected strongly, others knew that Meg had been baptised a Christian, and pleaded that whilst she might not deserve a proper Christian burial, she could not be denied a last resting-place near the house of the Lord. However, as a compromise she was buried away from other decent Christian souls, near a pathway, some yards from the church, and her burial took place at night, by torchlight.

But even then, the locals feared that in true witch fashion she would refuse to stay buried. During her lifetime poor Meg had been blamed for every small mishap in the district, and in the months after her death the villagers continued to suffer from the same problems; cows going dry, hens refusing to lay, horses going lame, and when some people began to report having seen Meg around the outskirts of the village, suspicions (and superstitions) were raised that the old witch was still up to her old tricks – except that now she was a ghost! Clearly, this couldn't be allowed to continue. So, in an attempt to keep the old witch where she should be, the villagers took the horrible decision to dig her body up and rebury it, head downwards, and then they placed a large boulder on top of the site to make absolutely sure she couldn't dig her way out again.

Meg Hilton may have been dead and buried for nearly three hundred years, but her legend lives on, and the stories are told today with a humour far removed from the fear they inspired centuries ago. One local woman remembers how she and other children from the local Brownie pack used to dance round the witchstone and spit on it.

The witchstone is still there to be seen by the pathway to the church. And children today, inspecting the stone, are still likely to be warned by locals not to get too close, just in case Meg reaches up and grabs them by the ankle!

The boulder or 'witchstone', marking Meg Hilton's grave in St Anne's churchyard.

THE EXORCISM OF HOBSTONE'S FARM

The very name 'Hobstone's Farm' is enough to evoke a romantic image of a stone-built country farm nestling tidily in the green rolling hills and fields of the countryside, the air full of the quiet sounds of faraway sheep and birdsong. However, on second thought, the name has more sinister connotations. Those who are at all versed in Northern folklore will recognise that the word Hob is the shortened form of 'hobgoblin', and is itself associated with mischievous dwarfs and elves. The terrifying science-fiction film *Quatermass and the Pit* also used the word in the name of the fictional London Underground station Hobbs Lane, the setting for the story.

The locals in Foulridge near Colne believe that the land on which Hobstones Farm is built, and the fields surrounding it, was in ancient times a burial ground. Their belief is not without foundation; the local lake, Lake Burwain, takes its name from ancient English words which mean 'burial place'. Traditionally such places were common breeding grounds for hobs; dwarves, elves and the like. Its no surprise then that the stone farm, which had imposed its presence on the English landscape for many centuries, should have taken on the name; 'Hobstones'. Nor should it be a surprise that the farm itself is the source of much local superstition; certain happenings there have left a deep impression on the neighbourhood, and on some of the farm's occupants in particular.

In the 1950's one tenant farmer was peacefully sitting on the outside lavatory when suddenly the door opened and he saw a small man standing there. The man, who was dressed like a monk, slowly extended his arm towards the farmer – or should we say the remains of his arm, which was horribly severed at the elbow, and still dripping blood. Then as suddenly as it came, the figure vanished, leaving the farmer bemused and frightened, still sitting there. Although the vision lasted for only a few seconds, the farmer managed to give a detailed description of the monk. Apparently he had been rather dwarfish in build, with a weather-beaten and somewhat twisted face.

As the weeks went by after the incident, and the farmer regained his nerve, he decided that either he had momentarily lost his mind or the whole episode had been down to someone playing some kind of macabre practical joke. But then the monk appeared again, and this time he was not the only witness – his wife was with him, and she watched with astonishment as the diminutive monk appeared quite suddenly in front of them, and slowly took a few steps in their direction, and then when the ghost was no more than a few feet away, it vanished in a moment.

This was no practical joke, the farmer realised, as he tried to comfort his wife, who was quite naturally upset by this horrific apparition. Over the ensuing weeks, their distress grew worse as the monk appeared more regularly, in a variety of places, both inside and outside the farm. Nothing they said or did seemed to help, and it seemed their only course of action was to leave the farm for good, giving up their living, and trying to make a new life for themselves elsewhere.

Twenty years later, Hobstones farm was taken over by the Berry family, who soon began to experience more than their share of strange experiences. It began with odd noises, as if someone was thumping the walls of the old stone farmhouse. Then, more terrifyingly, objects began to move of their own accord. On one occasion the washing machine was flung across the kitchen, along with a tray of eggs. It was odd enough that the heavy machine could move so far and so rapidly all on its own, but even odder was the fact that whilst all the white eggs in the tray had been broken by the impact, all the brown eggs were intact, and positioned in the tray in the shape of a cross . . .

The events continued, in many parts of the house. One time a leaded window was destroyed; on examination it appeared that the window had been pushed outwards, and the really inexplicable thing was that the glass had not shattered as one would expect, but seemed to have been ground into tiny pieces. On another occasion everyone in the family was brought rushing to the main entrance by the sound of loud and urgent banging on the door, but there was no one to be seen – and yet as they stood there the banging continued, as if the door was being pounded by a giant, invisible fist.

By now it was clear that the incidents were falling into a typical pattern of a 'classic' poltergeist – not that such a diagnosis was any help to the Berry family, who must have found it very difficult to live with the knowledge that something else very weird might happen at any moment. The case was also unusual because the experiences were lasting longer than the so-called 'normal' six to nine months. In fact the family continued to be plagued by similar uncanny events for some four years, and by 1974 they had reached the end of their tethers. They could not go on living like this; newspaper reports stated that at times the farmhouse's walls and ceilings were shaking so violently that it was feared the house would collapse. The reporters also decided that as there was no natural cause for such awful happenings, the farmhouse must have been invaded by demons . . .

The mention of devilish works only increased the panic surrounding the case. It was decided that as a last resort the Church of England should be consulted, and the Reverend Noel Hawthorn came to examine the farm and listen to the family's incredible stories. He decided that an exorcism was warranted, and according to Church rites, every room in the farmhouse was blessed with holy water, and the tormented spirits assumed to be responsible were banished from the place.

From that time, things began to quieten down, and life gradually – and thankfully – resumed its normal pace. Since then, the farmhouse has been demolished and the area redeveloped. However, if any future residents in that area suddenly begin to have strange experiences, it won't come as a surprise to many of the locals who still remember the time when demons infested Hobstones Farm . . .

LEVENS HALL

Five miles south of Kendal, Levens Hall and its beautiful gardens attract thousands of tourists every year. A major feature of the site is the seventeenth century topiary garden, designed by a Frenchman who was also gardener to James II. In daytime the garden is charming and restful, but at night the intricately cut designs take on an eerie and sinister appearance. It is enough to make the most hardened sceptic imagine all sorts of ghostly nightime visitors are lurking amongst the myriad pathways.

But Levens Hall and its gardens are indeed reputed to be haunted, and the stories are intriguing, for more than one group of scientific investigators have attested to some strange events. This story is based on the experiences of one such group of investigators.

Our research begins with the folklore. The tale is that sometime early in the eighteenth century a gypsy, weak and starving, called for alms at Levens Hall. She dragged herself along the drive, but having reached the main entrance to the Hall, was summarily turned away by the staff, who were affronted that a mere gypsy should dare to approach the Hall in this way. If she wanted help, she was told, she could go around the house to the back entrance. The poor woman was too weak to find the rear of the house, and collapsed and died where she lay. But before she died she cursed the family, saying that no man in the family would be succeeded by his own son, until a white fawn was born in the Hall's deer park, and the waters of the nearby River Kent ceased to flow.

For many generations the curse held true; the estate passed down the female line, but never from father to son. Then, in 1895 a pale-coloured fawn was born to one of the black Norwegian fallow deer which roamed the acres of park land, and that year also saw a severe winter which caused the Kent to freeze solid. The next year a boy was born to the Bagot family, and in 1913 this young man finally succeeded his father.

1946 saw the birth of Hal Bagot, the present owner of Levens Hall, and whilst he dismisses some of the ghostly legends associated with his ancestral home, he will admit that in the year of his own birth a white fawn was again born to a deer in the park – and again the Kent froze over. When his own first son was born, on December 12, 1981, the river was frozen solid, and another white fawn was born.

The River Kent flowing by Levens Hall: 'No man's son shall inherit from his father, until the Kent ceases to flow.'

The gypsy's shade is said to haunt the scene of her last tortured journey along the main drive to the house. Family members and friends have seen the Grey Lady, as she is known, and occasionally motorists on the nearby main road have told of their shock on thinking they have struck a woman on the road, only to find no trace of anyone on investigation.

The house itself is also haunted by a small black dog – several visitors to the Hall have reported seeing the cheerful little creature dash past them on the stairs and disappear into a bedroom, and they are amazed that on entering the room there is no sign of the animal. Over a decade ago a family posed for a photograph on the steps of the house, accompanied by a small black dog happily wagging his tail. The origin of this friendly ghost is a mystery – although the Bagots have owned many dogs, none of them fit the description of this small cheeky fellow.

Another frequent ghostly visitor to the Hall and its grounds is the Pink Lady, who appears at several locations dressed in a long dress and apron, and wearing a mob cap. She may have been a young servant at the Hall, held at the place by some emotional trauma – though no one has ever discovered who she might have been.

Our story now moves forward to 1992 when a group of ASSAP investigators staged a ghost hunt in the grounds of the house one late August night. As part of the experiment none of the team were told anything of the folklore about Levens Hall or its gardens, and they had come from far enough away not to have any local knowledge of the place. All the investigators approached the night – and the site – with a healthy scepticism.

The team's two women members, in particular, had no expectations, having already taken part in a similar experiment at a supposedly haunted property and gaining nothing but bags under their eyes and terminally cold feet.

The two women, Louise and Kate, were asked to observe events in the topiary garden, and for convenience they sat under two beautifully trimmed yew trees with circular seats around their trunks. They chose one of these trees as a base where they could leave their bags and coffee-flasks.

It was very peaceful, which they both remarked upon, but after a few minutes the mood changed and they both began to feel very sad, and independently felt the presence of a young woman, aged about twenty-two, dressed in white with a pink trim. Perhaps they had received a visit from the Pink Lady.... but that wasn't the only thing to happen under that particular tree.

Later in the night, another team left equipment on the bench around the tree and returned a few minutes later to find that both a still camera and a video camera had completely flat batteries – they had been fully charged before the vigil. The still camera had been used for twelve pictures, only two of which were later found to be properly exposed – the rest were ruined. The video camera, which had been left switched on, had only operated for 15 minutes of its usual hour and a half of charge.

The video recording offered no explanation of what had happened. It merely showed the investigators walking away from the camera, and then after a few minutes came the sound of a notebook's pages rustling. A notebook had been left on the bench, but there was very little breeze... After that there was nothing. No logical explanation for the flat batteries could be found, unless it was simply a coincidence. One point is worth mentioning here – there are many stories by investigators of normally well-behaved equipment behaving oddly at some haunted sites.

Later that same night Louise and Kate were standing on one of the wide garden pathways when Kate saw a flash of light against the dense hedge a few feet away. The flash resembled a camera flash, but was too localised, and both were sure there was no one on the other side of the hedge. Kate dashed through an archway cut through the greenery, calling out 'Hello?', but none of their colleagues were even close enough to hear her call, let alone to have taken a flash photograph. On further investigation it seemed unlikely that the light was caused by a camera flash, as the hedge was very dense and it would be impossible for a light to penetrate such thick foliage.

Louise and Kate continued to patrol the area, and their next stop was a small circular garden, in the centre of which was an enormous stone urn. It was a pretty scene and so they switched off their torches to view the place by starlight. After a few quiet moments, Louise suddenly saw the urn lit up as if by another brief flash of light – but again, there was no other camera or torch user in the area.

Later in the night Kate and Louise were stationed in the area to the front of the house, and as everything seemed quiet, they began a systematic examination of their allotted area, making their way together down the lawn towards the picnic area at the far end. The closer they came, the more uncomfortable they felt, but they continued to walk until they had gone as far as they could. Turning to come back to the house, they noticed that the oppressive feeling diminished, at last disappearing altogether. It wasn't until the team were debriefed in the early morning that it was discovered that these feelings of oppression had been experienced in the exact place that the Grey Lady is supposed to appear and walk towards the house, replaying her final journey.

Strange lights, a 'presence', and dark sensations in the Grey Lady's haunting-place – all this would be enough for most people, but Louise had one final peculiar experience that night, whilst she and Kate were following the other four investigators back to their cars. It was dark and all torches were switched off, and the team veered off the pathway to the left to reach the car park. All except one. Louise saw one of the team pull away and instead of veering to the left, carry straight on down the path. They had been specifically asked to avoid that area of the house, near the kitchen, for fear of rousing the family dogs who slept there. She waited for the barking to start – and then she realised that their party was complete and the figure she had seen was not one of their team after all . . .

Levens Hall near Kendal.

ALICE THE GHOST

Some years ago, I (Melanie Warren) had some very strange experiences in my own home in the seaside town of St. Annes. At the time I was not in the least bit curious about the paranormal, but over a period of three years I began to run out of rational explanations for everything that happened. Maybe it was just a string of coincidences, but by far the easiest explanation is that I shared my house with a ghost.

At that time my children were only toddlers and I was a full-time housewife and mother. Our house in St Anne's was a large family house with three stories. We lived very comfortably in the top two stories and rented out the ground floor as a shop. My husband worked late into the evenings, and my children were always in bed early, so I spent many hours alone. I didn't mind, as the old house was very friendly and I never felt lonely. In fact there were times when I could have sworn I wasn't even alone!

One evening, when I was sewing quietly in the room between the lounge and the kitchen, I had the strangest feeling that someone was standing behind me. Of course, when I looked, there was no one there and I put it down to imagination. Then it happened again a few weeks later, and again a week or so after that.

I didn't tell anyone about what had happened, because I had not really seen or heard anything definite. It was just an impression that someone, a woman, was in the room behind me. I have no idea why I thought it was a woman – that's just the way it felt. But the whole thing seemed so trivial I had no problem forgetting about it.

A couple of months later, a friend and I decided to visit a local medium, Jay Norton, just for fun. Imagine my surprise when Jay asked me if I was aware of a 'friend', or ghost, in my house. She went on to describe a scene where she saw me alone in a room, whipping my head round quickly as if I expected to see someone standing behind me – which was precisely what had happened.

My astonishment must have been obvious to Jay, who spent some time persuading me that my 'ghost' was just a lady who had lived in the house many years ago. Jay said that the lady didn't want to frighten me, but she just liked to pop in from time to time to see how the old place was doing.

I still didn't tell anyone else about my so-called 'ghost'. I didn't see the point, as I had no real evidence. Then later that year, Carole, the woman who ran the shop on the ground floor of our house, also expressed an interest in visiting Jay. Although I was never convinced by Jay's statements about the spirit world, or where her information came from, I had mentioned to Carole how interesting Jay's readings were. I personally thought much of the so-called evidence she had given me might have been obtained telepathically, rather than spiritually, but that was interesting enough in itself.

Although Carole was interested in the procedure, and we had talked about mediums at some length, I felt she was a little nervous about it, and so I had never mentioned our ghost – I thought that might be too much for her. I accompanied Carole to her appointment with Jay, armed with a notebook to record whatever Jay had to say.

I had booked Carole's appointment under my own name, which meant Jay could not possibly have done any prior research about Carole. I was therefore surprised when Jay again began talking about a ghost, asking if Carole had ever felt that someone was in her shop, perhaps when she was working late at night . . . Carole denied ever having felt a thing, but Jay went on to describe the ghost in the same way she had described it to me; a lady who had once lived in the building, just popping back to see how the old place was doing. She

109

said the lady's name was Alice.

After the initial surprise, the sceptic in me reasoned that Jay must simply be a very observant lady and adept at putting two and two together; earlier in the reading she had deduced that Carole was a shop-owner, and it was a short step to guessing that Carole's shop was the one below my home. I thought it couldn't be true, as I still didn't believe there were such things as ghosts.

Then a few months later, I became convinced that my small son saw Alice the Ghost walk through a wall. He was less than two years old, far too young to verbalise what he had seen – but his actions left me in no doubt. It happened one afternoon when we were walking down the hall. Ahead of us was a blank wall, behind which was the dining area of the kitchen. Suddenly my baby son stopped dead, pointing urgently at the wall and jabbering at me. I asked him what was the matter, and he ran to the wall and banged on it with both fists. Then he went round to the other side of the wall and banged on it again. He looked at me for a response, and then repeated the performance several times, all the while jabbering at me in baby-talk.

He was obviously distressed, wanting to tell me something but unable to do so. His actions were so unusual that I felt he must have seen our 'friend' walk through that wall, but I was unwilling to ask him if this was the case for fear of putting ideas into his head. However, as he grew more and more frustrated at his inability to explain himself, I finally asked, 'Did you see a lady walk through the wall?' He nodded violently and jumped into my arms for a cuddle, relieved that finally I understood.

The one thing that really puzzled me was why Alice the Ghost should choose to walk through a wall in such a scary way, when Jay had assured me she didn't want to frighten anyone. Or maybe her appearance was like a kind of video-recording, walking through a wall which had perhaps contained a door in her time.

A while later we moved from that house. The man who bought the property, Bill, was an acquaintance of ours, so it was no surprise when he phoned me one afternoon – until he explained he'd phoned to ask about the ghost! He told me how he had been regularly working late, in the room between the lounge and the kitchen, and several times had been convinced that a woman was standing there watching him. He had felt exactly how I had felt, in exactly the same place!

Bill had never given much thought to ghosts before, but these 'feelings' had been so strong that he'd mentioned them to Carole in the shop and was intrigued when she told him he'd better give me a call. Carole had said nothing previously, because like the rest of us, she didn't believe in ghosts.

Some months later I was in the area and popped in to see Carole. After a few moments Bill arrived and invited me upstairs to see the changes he'd made to my old home. The first thing I noticed was that a previously blank wall now contained a door. Naturally I commented on this, and was told that Bill's architect had obtained the original plans for the building, and had simply replaced a door which had always been there. It seemed like the last piece in the puzzle, for the door was in exactly the same spot where my son had banged his fists that day. The very place where Alice the ghost had walked through the wall!

As a postscript, one evening another medium came to my new home and announced to the assembled company – about six of us – that a lady by the name of Alice wished to be remembered to me. My friends, who had all heard about Alice the Ghost, found this hilarious, especially when the medium observed that as Alice was not a relative of mine and had nothing to do with my new home, she hoped I knew who Alice was. After the merriment subsided, once again I was left with the old questions. Was it just a coincidence? Or was it telepathy? Or was it, after all, my old friend Alice the Ghost, just popping in to say hello?

BLENKINSOPP CASTLE

The story of Sir Bryan de Blenkinsopp and the White Lady of Blenkinsopp Castle has all the hallmarks of a medieval romance: a brave Knight, his fair Lady, a castle on a hill, and chests of gold. The gold was especially important, because Sir Bryan's personal fortune made him one of the richest men in the North. Minstrels' songs paid tribute to his bravery, and he basked in the admiration of the womenfolk. His only fault was his love of money, and it was this failing which led to his downfall. His private fortune may have been enormous, but he was never satisfied – like a true miser, he always wanted more.

Those around him were made well aware of Sir Bryan's attitude to money when one of his fellow knights married. During the wedding celebrations, when toasts were flowing thick and fast, a toast was proposed 'to Bryan de Blenkinsopp and his Ladylove'. Sir Bryan got to his feet and drunkenly pronounced that he would never marry any woman unless she brought with her a chest of gold heavier than ten strong men could carry. The wedding guests were shocked into silence by this blatant display of avarice, and Sir Bryan was shamed into leaving the wedding party – in fact, he left the country and stayed away for several years.

When he eventually returned, he brought with him a dusky-skinned wife and her several attendants – and she in her turn brought a box of gold so heavy that it took twelve of Sir Bryan's men to carry it into the castle. And for a while everyone was happy; Bryan's wishes for his marriage had been fulfilled, his followers rejoiced at his return, and he was once again famous for his fortune.

But the local people didn't know what to make of Sir Bryan's wife. No one knew who she was or where she had come from – some even said the mysterious dark woman wasn't a woman at all – she was a demon, sent with her money by the Devil, to lead Sir Bryan astray. Their suspicions were fuelled when they heard that Sir Bryan and his wife had been quarrelling, because she and her attendants had hidden her dowry chest of gold and refused to tell Sir Bryan where it was. Finally Sir Bryan left the castle in a great hurry, and didn't come back. Days and weeks passed, with no sign of him. His young wife was devastated, and sent men out to scour the country and search abroad for her husband, but a whole year passed with no word. At last Sir Bryan's wife took her attendants and set out to search for him herself.

Neither Sir Bryan nor his beautiful dark-skinned wife were ever seen again – alive, that is. But many years later people were saying that the Lady must have died, because her ghost had been seen in Blenkinsopp Castle. The tales suggested that she had come back to haunt the place because she was herself haunted by the memory of the chest of gold – the cause of all her troubles. She would not be able to rest until the chest was found and removed from the castle.

Centuries after their strange disappearance, the castle had fallen into a sad state of disrepair, although parts of it still housed labourers on the estate. Among their number was the gardener, who lived in two castle rooms with his wife and children. One black night, the air was rent by a terrible scream. It came from the room in which the children were sleeping. The gardener and his wife rushed in, to find their little son trembling after a terrible nightmare. He said that a lady dressed in white sat on his bed beside him, kissed his cheek and begged him to go with her to a secret place where she would show him – and give him – a chest of gold. When he said he was too frightened to go, she took him in her arms and would have lifted him up, had he not screamed and woken his parents. He eventually calmed down and settled to sleep, but was tormented by the vision three more times before his parents decided to move him into another room. After that, he was not bothered by the White Lady again.

The oldest records of this story mention that the other labourers living in the castle were severely shaken by this episode – everyone knew the legend about the White Lady, but as it was centuries old, no one had really believed it. It could be said that the stories had simply caused the young boy to have nightmares . . .

When the boy grew up he emigrated to Canada and did well for himself. He always claimed that his experience was not a simple nightmare – it had been as real as any experience he'd had since. He said that when he thought about it, he could still remember the imprint of the Lady's cold lips pressed against his cheek . . .

The years rolled on to the twentieth century, when another story fuelled the legend of the buried treasure. A strange lady arrived at a village next to the castle, settled in for a long stay at a local inn, and then left some weeks later. It was only to be expected that her presence would cause some talk: who was she? What was she doing there? The landlady knew, and although she had been sworn to secrecy by her mysterious visitor, she found the whole thing too exciting and soon her story had been whispered from one villager to the next.

The visitor had been plagued by a strange dream, in which she had seen chests of gold lying in a castle vault. Passing through this area for the first time in her life, she had come across Blenkinsopp Castle, and with a shock had recognised it as the scene of her dream. She had tried to gain permission to search the castle, but the owners were away and so she had decided to stay for a while, until they returned. Very soon it was clear to the woman that her story was out, and she left the area – perhaps through embarrassment. She never did return.

Blenkinsopp Castle is now owned by Michael Simpson, who has his own stories to tell about the place. At the time of writing, it has been his home for forty years. He came to live in the castle as a boy of nine, with his parents and eighteen-year-old brother Gordon. He was as thrilled as any young boy could be, to be living in a real castle, with stone-built walls and long mysterious corridors! But one night he had an experience which has stayed with him all his life as something he just cannot explain.

Late one night he was lying in bed with a full moon streaming through the uncurtained window. He heard footsteps coming along the main corridor outside, but they were strangely slow: plod . . . plod . . . plod . . . He thought it must be his brother Gordon, tired and back from his night out performing with the Scottish Country Dance Band he belonged to. The footsteps carried on, down the corridor until they reached the small corridor which led to Michael's room. Then they started again, coming towards his bedroom door. By the moonlight, Michael saw the doorknob begin to turn. It turned as far as it could turn, but the door did not open, and after what seemed like an hour the knob snapped back into place as whoever had been turning it released the pressure. There was an eerie atmosphere in the room, but Michael tried not to think of ghosts – as the footsteps retreated down the corridor, he decided that Gordon must have had a few drinks too many and had momentarily mistaken Michael's room for his own. The next morning young Michael commented to his mother that Gordon had come in very late – it must have been about four in the morning. 'Oh no,' she told him, 'he didn't come home at all; he stayed the night with the Bandleader . . . '

When Michael was sixteen, he made friends with a joiner working on the castle estate; a fascinating old chap who was in his eighties. He had heard all the tales about the White Lady, and told Michael that there was a tunnel, hidden in the East Wall, which was supposed to be the entrance to the secret vault where the Lady had hidden her treasure. The old man had served his apprenticeship with a mason, and the mason had served his own time in renovating the East Wall of the castle, which is when the entrance had been found in 1880 . . .

The wall itself was about eight feet thick, and whilst the men were working on the restoration, they came across a section where the workmanship looked suspicious, as if this particular section had been put together very hastily. They began to remove the large stones and found behind them a passage. One brave man volunteered to explore the passage, but going underground was risky; all the coal pits in the area were plagued with Black Damp, a noxious gas, and there was no telling whether pockets of it wouldn't be lurking down this passage as well. At last someone brought a gas-detector in the form of a canary, (common in coal mines at that time: if there was gas, the canary literally dropped off its perch!) and the search commenced.

The chap was gone for some minutes, and when he came stumbling back again he described how he had walked along the low, narrow passageway, down a flight of stairs, along another passage to a badly-rotted door which was hanging off its hinges. To the side of him the staircase spiralled steeply down, but he could go no further – the canary he had brought with him was dead. Not surprisingly the story spread like wildfire around the village that up at the castle they'd found the entrance to the White Lady's treasure chamber, and in later days two more attempts were made to explore the tunnel further and find out if there really was any treasure down there. But each time the Black Damp forced them back again. In the end, enthusiasm waned and the entrance was sealed up again for safety.

Michael has never actually seen the White Lady, and doesn't know anyone who has. A ghostly lady *was* seen about twenty years ago, by

Michael's brother and two other men, but she wasn't white . . .

In the mid-seventies it was decided to convert the old outbuildings into a pub: the Blenkinsopp Castle Inn, complete with function room. One evening Michael's brother Gordon came into the pub at seven to open up, and was surprised to see a woman customer already standing at the end of the bar. But as he looked at her more closely, she simply disappeared. A little later a young barman was sitting down in the bar, from where he could see into the function room. He too saw a woman – who walked straight through the wall. Finally, at the end of the evening, whilst the chief barman was emptying the till, he had the sudden sensation that someone was watching him from behind, and when he turned around he found a woman standing there, looking over his shoulder. Then she turned, and walked away – straight through the wall.

The next morning, one of the men confessed what he had seen, and the other two were relieved to relate their own experiences. And only a week later, there was another story to add to the collection when a cleaner, working early one morning, glanced up to see a woman standing behind the bar. For a second she thought it was Michael's wife, until she spoke and got no response – and then saw the woman walk away through the wall . . . The one thing all four people agreed on was that the ghostly woman wasn't the Lady in White – because she had been dressed in Elizabethan robes.

It would be nice to be able to say that Blenkinsopp Castle has many ghosts, but sadly that doesn't seem to be true – at least, not any more. Michael Simpson recalls that in the past there were many occasions when he felt a definite presence in his bedroom, and the castle itself seemed to have a unique atmosphere. But for the last ten years everything in the castle has been quiet: no White Lady, no Elizabethan Lady, no strange dreams or nightmares. The tunnel is still there – Michael has always intended to open it up once last time and explore it for himself, before sealing it forever with stone and hot lime.

It seems odd that a legend which has lasted so long and with so many stories to give it credence has not already led to a complete search of the tunnel, with the excavators armed with oxygen bottles and flashlights instead of canaries and lamps. But the locals seem in no hurry to venture into the castle's depths, buried treasure or no. Perhaps they've learned a lesson from Sir Bryan, who had the biggest fortune in the North, and still couldn't find happiness.

MOTHER SHIPTON

In 1687 a scholar by the name of Mr Head, known for recording the lives of famous people, came across the intriguing story of Mother Shipton. She was reputed to have been a witch with the gift of prophecy. She had been dead for a hundred years, yet her reputation lived on in tales passed from Yorkshire village to village, about her life and the things she had said and done. Although a popular belief in witches was still widespread in late seventeenth century England – in fact women accused of being witches were still occasionally being tried and executed – Mr Head was an educated man, and well aware of how such legends grow. He was not satisfied with merely writing down the stories the countryfolk were all too willing to relate. Storytelling was a popular form of evening entertainment, and tales lost nothing in the telling around the kitchen hearths of Yorkshire. No; Mr Head wanted to dig for what truth there was about this remarkable lady, and he determined to search for as long as it might take to find it.

He pored over old manuscripts and records, but for a long time could find no mention of Mother Shipton. . . . until at last he met a gentleman who told him that he had in his keeping several 'ancient writings' in which he might find what he was looking for. Unfortunately the papers he was shown were indeed very old, and the passage of time had affected them badly. They were almost illegible and would have crumbled, had not Mr Head known of a good remedy for the problem. He gathered a crop of oak apples – the bright-coloured spongy balls that form on the leaf-bud of oaks, and which are also known as galls – from local woodland, and beat and crushed them as well as he could. He then set them to steep in some good white wine, and having left them for several days, distilled the concoction

120

and collected the resulting liquid. With this he carefully dampened the old pages, and found the words coming to life before his eyes, as easily readable as the day they were written. At last he was able to read the stories of Mother Shipton.

Her name was Ursula Southiel, and she was born in Knaresborough on July 6th, 1488. She was described as a particularly ugly child, with a big crooked body and a frightful face – but in compensation for her physical deformity she grew into a young woman of uncanny intelligence. Her personality was so pleasant that a young builder by the name of Toby Shipton fell in love with her, and asked her to be his wife. But the marriage did not last long – no one knows exactly why, although it is probable that Toby died after just a few years. Mother Shipton lived alone from that time on, and gained a reputation for being a harmless sort of witch, able to predict small things about people's lives.

Such small prophecies were probably the result of her watching people with intelligence and drawing conclusions they would have drawn themselves, if they'd only had her common sense. But soon she began to make larger predictions about world affairs, and it is for this that she is best remembered.

Much of the recording of Mother Shipton's prophesies is owed to her contemporary, Mr Besly, a shop owner who would frequently close his business in the afternoon and pay her a visit to discover what new predictions she could come up with. Many of her sayings are in the form of rhymes, which, some scholars suspect, are not Mother Shipton's original words – perhaps Mr Besly or someone like him was responsible for re-stating them in this fashion, to add to their mystery. Some of her predictions were seen to come true within a few years; others took hundreds of years.

For example, one of the rhymes seems to refer to the Thames

Tunnel, which was built by the great Victorian engineer, Brunel, more than 260 years after Mother Shipton's death. The tunnel was the first of its kind, and was so difficult and expensive to cut under water that it took 18 years to complete. It also flooded five times during construction. After the second war the tunnel was taken over by London Underground and now forms part of the underground line from Wapping to Rotherhithe.

A year after the Thames Tunnel was completed, in 1843, Blackwell's Magazine pointed out that on a visit to Wapping, Mother Shipton had made a peculiar reference:

When below the Thames' bed
Shall be seen the furnace red,
When its bottom shall drop out,
Making hundreds swim about,
Where fish had never swum,
Then shall doleful tidings come

During the construction of the tunnel, there were five eruptions at the cutting face between 1827 and 1838. Each time the Thames broke through, the workforce literally had to swim for their lives back to the tunnel entrance. Sadly, there were several deaths. There is a remarkable correlation between the episodes of the tunnel floodings and Mother Shipton's words, uttered over 250 years before.

Another most remarkable story concerns Mother Shipton's prophecy about Cardinal Wolsey. When she heard that Henry was about to become King Henry the Eighth and Cardinal Wolsey would be taking up a position in York, she said, *'Cardinal Wolsey should never be at Yorke.'*

This came to the attention of Henry, who sent the Duke of Suffolk, Lord Darcy and Sir Thomas Percy to visit her. They enlisted the help of Mr Besly, who gave them plain clothes so Mother Shipton would not suspect their high positions. They asked Mother Shipton to explain her statement, and eventually she clarified what she had said like this: '*I said he might see Yorke, but never come at it.*'

Her prophecy came true, for after Wolsey had been banished by Henry the Eighth to the York diocese, he stayed at a town called Cawood, to make himself ready for his entry into York. From Cawood he could actually see the city of York in the distance – but he never made it through the city gates. In September 1530, he was arrested by the Earl of Northumberland on the orders of the King, and was taken back to London on a charge of high treason. Wolsey died on the journey in Leicester before he could be tried . . . and Mother Shipton's prophecy came true.

Mother Shipton made a great number of prophecies, and the two we have chosen about the Thames Tunnel and the Wolsey affair are among the most interesting. Many of the others are little more than pure legend, as is her alleged association with the Rollwright stones near Chipping Norton, in Oxfordshire.

The legend says that an ambitious warrior knight was determined to make the whole country his own, and had progressed north as far as the borders of Warwickshire. Mother Shipton was staying in the area – in fact, the story says she gave her name to the village which is now known as Shipton-Under-Wychwood – and she swore the knight should not progress any further. Early one morning, she confronted the knight and four of his fellow knights, and exclaimed; *"Rise up hill! Stand fast stone! King of England thou shalt be none!"* And with these words she waved her arm, and the knights were turned to stone. They can be seen still – the five large stones known as the Whispering Knights, standing gauntly in a circle known as the Rollright stones.

Mother Shipton's last prediction concerned her own death. She called her friends together and told them exactly when she would die. She passed away in dignity, in her own bed, aged 73, in 1561. After her death a monument was erected to her memory between the villages of Clifton and Shipton. Her epitaph reads:

Here lies she who never lied,
Whose skill often has been tried,
Her prophecies shall still survive
And ever keep her name alive.

THE VAMPIRE OF CROGLIN

Amelia Cranswell sat in her comfortable armchair darning by the light of a solitary candle. It was not easy – it had taken months of perseverance for her to get used to such close work by such feeble and sputtering light. A far cry from her adventures abroad with her two brothers. She sighed, remembering the happy times they had had. It was late, the clock had just struck eleven o'clock – no wonder her eyes were feeling gritty and tired.

She felt so weary, a nineteen-year-old girl unused to the demands of running Squire Fisher's large house. She had no wish to return home to her own village, however, as the superstitious villagers there regarded her family as harbingers of evil. Every time they returned from a jaunt abroad, any disasters in the village were somehow attributed to them. At least here in Croglin, most of the locals were friendly. The only thing which worried Amelia was an awareness that her youthful beauty had attracted the unwelcome attentions of several young men.

However, there were some disturbing rumours in the area. These stories had so upset Squire Fisher that he had taken his wife south to Guildford. He had left his godsons, Amelia's brothers, as deputies in his absence.

A few years previously, in 1730, a gypsy had been wrongly accused of sheep-stealing and had been lynched by an angry mob. His kinsmen pronounced a curse on all those responsible that 'pestilences, horrors and devilish happenings' would befall them. Within twelve months villagers were reporting a ghostly hound who appeared on the fell and killed several sheep, yet could never be caught.

125

Croglin Hall in Cumberland.

There was also the much older story, that the nearby church at Renwick was home to a strange and terrifying creature. When the church was being rebuilt, a 'great winged creature' had flown out from a demolished wall and subjected the builders to a terrifying attack. One of them, braver than the others, had grabbed a branch and beaten the monster back into the foundations of the church, where his workmates had quickly bricked it up. His actions had been considered so valiant that he had been relieved of paying tithes for life. However, no one was certain that the creature was dead . . . There were also persistent rumours of a beast called a vampire. It was supposed to attack women and children, draining them of their blood and eventually killing them.

Amelia, a sensible girl, considered the stories to be just superstitious nonsense. She shut her eyes for a few minutes to rest them, and listened to the soothing sounds of the pleasant summer night drifting through her window, a far cry from the stories of vampires and winged monsters . . . She began to drift off to sleep.

"Get up," a voice hissed. She awoke with a start. A hand was over her mouth and an arm around her neck. In a panic she flailed helplessly trying to free herself but her attacker was too strong.

"Get up," the voice hissed again. "And if you make one noise, I will break your neck". The arm tightened itself around her neck to show that he meant business and she gingerly raised herself from the chair. "Now, lets move across towards the bed."

"No!" she gasped and desperately tried to pull away. But by now the arm around her neck was excruciatingly painful and it was difficult to breathe. She wondered what choices she had, whether to submit to this animal intent on rape, or to somehow struggle and try to wake the rest of the house.

There was not much fight left in her as she could scarcely breathe and had little strength to use against her powerful attacker.

She decided to signal her submission, and so he started to drag her across the room towards the bed. As he forced her along and there seemed no hope of escape, the unexpected happened – the hallway clock outside her room chimed loudly. The sound made her jump, but it also surprised her attacker, who loosened his grip on her neck. Realising her chance, she pushed with all of her fading strength. She managed to push him into her sewing table and with a huge crash the thing toppled over. Her attacker lost his hold . . .

The next thing she remembered was finding herself in bed in full daylight and old Mrs Fell from the nearby farm bringing in a breakfast tray.

It then took Amelia over three months of recuperation to get over her ordeal. Her brothers were most kind and insisted on taking her to Switzerland, making clear that neither they nor she would return to England until she was better.

In the end it was not Switzerland that helped her recover, it was her anger and resentment at being attacked in her own home. Croglin was not the prettiest of country houses, but they had paid for the lease, and she had regarded it as her house, and her sanctuary.

What really made her return to England with her brothers was the desire to catch her attacker, and she thought she knew exactly how to do it.

So here she was, back again by the fireside in her bedroom, sewing by the light of a candle. But this time she was prepared. She lay back in her seat and closed her eyes, thinking she would not doze, for she was alert to the slightest sound, any noise which could signal the return of her unknown attacker. Her eyelids were heavy through lack of sleep. The clock struck 3 o'clock and she decided to wait another half hour before retiring to bed.

With a start she awoke, not sure how long she had dozed. She strained her ears for any noise, but it was completely quiet both inside and out. Then suddenly she heard stealthy footfalls behind her and she spun round in terror. Her attacker was coming towards her – she could just make out his shape in the darkness.

"Edward!", she screamed, wondering where her brothers were and why they were not playing their part. The figure came closer, and in fear she sprang out of her chair and backed away towards the door. Then, thank God, she heard her brother's voice behind her. "Stop right there and let me get a look at you."

The dark shape backed away towards the window. Edward shouted, "Stop or I shoot!". The intruder broke into a run and Edward fired – Amelia jumped as the shot rang out from behind her. The flare from Edward's musket lit up the scene and left an image with her that would remain all her life. The flash showed why the intruder had been difficult to see – he wore a long black cloak which obscured most of his features. But as he clambered through the open window he turned, and Amelia saw his face – the face of a old man. She was positive she had never seen him before.

Next she heard the man cursing and a dull thud as he hit the ground, some ten feet below. Amelia and Edward rushed to the window in time to see the cloaked shape crossing the carriageway and moving into the shadow of a nearby copse. Edward pointed to a smear of blood on the window sill and exclaimed, "I've hit him!".

They both rushed downstairs, and Amelia quickly lit a lantern while Edward grabbed another loaded musket. They rushed to the copse and tried to pick up the trail of the intruder. They were unlucky as there was little blood to be found, and their lantern was not good enough to help them pick their way through the tangled undergrowth. For the moment, the intruder had got away.

Next morning, they rode into the village to raise the alarm, and to find someone who owned a tracker dog. Three good men from the village turned out, and the five of them set off on the trail of the intruder. Edward went ahead with the dog, which had been given the scent from a smear of the blood on Amelia's window sill. They followed the trail through the copse, which in daylight was much less dangerous.

The dog, sniffing and whining all the way, led them to the local graveyard at the edge of the village. The dog took the hunters into the middle of the graveyard, where to their horror they found that several graves had been opened and the coffins lifted and laid on the ground.

At the sight of the sundered graves, the three men from the village muttered and backed away. Amelia realised why – the sight of the coffins had awakened their fears about the vampire.

In the meantime the dog was in a frenzy. Edward freed her and she rushed at one of the coffins and started scratching frantically at the lid . . .

Edward pushed the lid aside, and resting in the coffin was one of the recently buried men from the village, with blood smeared over his face and a wound in one of his legs. Edward shouted "There's the bullet wound", but then had to turn away, overcome with nausea at the sight and stench of the corpse.

But Amelia had her mission – she was determined to make sure the corpse was indeed her attacker so she could live in peace again. She went over to the coffin and examined it closely. She quickly realised that this corpse had nothing to do with her troubles. She remembered the flash of the musket and the image of the intruder's face which was burned into her mind's eye – the face of an old man, heavily lined and wrinkled. The face of this corpse was youthful, unlined. This was a fake, the corpse deliberately tampered with to make them all think that it was the body of the attacker.

She looked at the three villagers, big men normally unafraid of anything, but now obviously very frightened. She looked at Edward who was trying to restrain the dog, and made her decision. The crowd in the graveyard was increasing in size as the rest of the village came to see what all the noise was about. A quick decision had to be made. Amelia guessed that her attacker would never return to repeat his molestations, having gone to such lengths to lead his pursuers astray. Yet the villagers were scared almost out of their wits by the thought that this body was that of a vampire, who could rise again under the cloak of night and roam the neighbourhood. She felt she should now go along with their belief in the vampire, and deal with it in the traditional manner.

She shouted to her audience, which by now had swollen to include the rest of the village who'd come to see what was going on: "This is the body of the man that attacked me – here, see the shot from Edward's musket.", and then pointed down at the corpse's bloody leg. The villagers nodded nervously. "We must drive a stake through his heart to prevent any more happenings" she continued.

She then walked over to the pathway and found a strong piece of broken coffin wood, and a large stone. With all her courage and strength, she rammed the stick into the chest of the corpse, battering it in deeper with the stone until she had pierced its heart.

That is how the story of Amelia Cranswell ends, a legend with no written evidence to back up the tale. Interestingly, Sir Arthur Conan Doyle came across the story while researching *The Hound of the Baskervilles*, and Bram Stoker used it for inspiration when creating the Count Dracula story which we all know today.

But there is an interesting postscript to the legend . . . In 1734 the body of an old man was found floating down the local river Eden. One can speculate that Amelia had possibly found her real intruder, and had at last gained revenge for her awful experiences.

Sadly, the original Croglin village no longer exists. Shortly after 1734, the village went into decline, and the buildings were left to crumble and decay.

THE BRONTËS

It was in 1820 that Patrick Brontë and his wife brought their son and five daughters to live in the large Georgian house on the edge of the moors. It was a fine house, despite the sobering view of the graveyard beyond the garden wall, and the imposing church beyond that. But this house was a parsonage, and so its outlook was wholly appropriate. When Patrick watched his young family settling in and working at their studies, or at play, he cannot have guessed how tragic their lives were to be.

The church at the end of the parsonage garden.

The first disaster struck when they lost their mother the following year. The eldest child was only eight years old, and although their Aunt Elizabeth moved in to look after them, she was no real substitute for a mother's love. Tragedy struck again when the girls were sent away to school. Conditions there were so bad that Maria and Elizabeth became ill and died, and consequently Charlotte and Emily were rapidly removed from the place. None of the children ever quite recovered from the shock of losing their sisters.

For the next five years, Charlotte, Emily, Anne and Branwell were educated at home. When not at their lessons, they spent their time in fantasy, inventing imaginary kingdoms and writing about them in miniature books, small enough for their toy soldiers to read. Perhaps their fantasy world was safer than the real one, where mothers and sisters could sicken and die, but it was this sad childhood which produced, in one family, three of the greatest novelists England has ever produced: Charlotte, Emily and Anne Brontë.

One of the few pleasures in their lives was to walk on the moors around their home in Haworth, and the landscape provided them with the inspiration for many of their stories. Their favourite stroll was along a two-mile path to a place where a waterfall cascaded down a sheer cliff-side, providing nourishment for plants and flowers which normally struggled to survive on the windswept moors. Within sight of this romantic place was a brooding house known as Top Withins, and it's easy to imagine the girls dreaming about who might live there and what romantic events might befall them. Indeed, it was this house which Emily described so vividly in her novel, *Wuthering Heights:*

Pure, bracing ventilation they must have up there at all times, indeed; one may guess the power of the north wind blowing over the edge, by the excessive slant of a few stunted firs at

the end of the house; and by a range of gaunt thorns all
stretching their limbs one way, as if craving alms of the sun.
Happily, the architect had foresight to build it strong: the
narrow windows are deeply set in the wall, and the corners
defended with large jutting stones.

Another house in the area was the model for the Hall in Anne's novel, *The Tenant Of Wildfell Hall*. Frail Anne, the youngest child, was not happy away from home and her three years as a governess at Blake Hall were among the unhappiest of her short life. *Wildfell Hall*, written in 1848, was a thin disguise for Blake Hall, and her experiences there were also the basis for her earlier novel *Agnes Grey*. By 1849 Anne was dead of TB, aged just thirty.

Charlotte was undeniably the strongest of the sisters, both physically and mentally, but her strength must have been tested severely as she watched her brother Branwell die at the age of thirty-two after a wild, intemperate short life. Her sister Emily died three months later of TB, aged thirty-one, and six months later Anne had also succumbed. Charlotte survived them all for a few more years. She married her father's curate in 1854, but died several months later, pregnant with her first child.

As one explores the parsonage, which still holds furniture and decorations owned and used by the Brontës, it is easy to imagine that the family has just stepped out for a moment and will be back presently. Patrick's study holds the piano which Emily loved to play, and in the kitchen stands the table where she would make bread, and in the dining room is the sofa where she died. At the base of the staircase is the Grandfather clock which Patrick would wind each night on his way to bed, and upstairs is the nursery where the children would write their stories. One would think that such tragic lives would leave some tangible traces behind them; a feeling of presence, a sensation of being watched – at the very least, an atmosphere of sadness. But there are no ghosts in this house.

Charlotte Brontë has never been seen anywhere since her death. Unlike her siblings, her life gave her the chance to fulfil herself in every way, even if she was young when she died. Perhaps this is the reason why she rests in relative peace.

Anne has allegedly been seen once – but not in Haworth or anywhere near it. When Blake Hall was demolished, its wonderful wooden staircase was bought by an American lady, a Mrs Gladys Topping, who had it shipped to her home in Long Island. To her delight, after the staircase had been installed, Mrs Topping saw a phantom woman walking up the stairs; she described her as wearing a long Victorian skirt, and having light-brown hair and blue eyes. There was no doubt in Mrs Topping's mind that her staircase had brought with it the ghost of Anne Brontë.

Back in Haworth, Emily Brontë is said to haunt The Weavers Restaurant, less than a hundred yards away from the parsonage where she grew up. It is said that she appears every year on December 19, the anniversary of her death. On this date in 1966, the owner of the restaurant saw the small figure for the first time, dressed in a crinoline, smiling and carrying a wicker basket. She walked in front of him to the place where the staircase had once been, and began to climb to the bedroom above. Her face was very familiar to the restaurant owner, who had seen it many times, in the family portrait which was painted by Emily's brother Branwell, and which still hangs in the parsonage museum.

Whilst the parsonage itself may hold no ghosts, the moorland around the village of Haworth is awash with memories. The house, Top Withins, the model for *Wuthering Heights*, still stands and can be seen from the 'Brontë Waterfall', alone and brooding on the hilltop. If you take the walk to the waterfall, it's difficult not to recall the final pages of *Wuthering Heights*, where Heathcliff, having died, was laid to rest in the windswept moorland – but did not rest . . . Those who lived thereabouts swore he walked abroad, and one child said he had seen a man and a woman embracing each other . . . If your walk along this path should be in the autumn, particularly in an evening or the early afternoon, you might not see Heathcliff, but take careful note of who you do pass on the way. For Emily, the inventor of these ghosts, is said to walk this way, drifting along 'with her head bowed deep in thought'.

The parsonage at Haworth.

SKULL HOUSES

Several stately homes in the North have some rather grisly ornamentation – in the form of human skulls. Each of these houses can provide a colourful legend to explain the presence of their particular skull, and whilst there is probably some truth to them, the original story is lost in the mists of time and now we can do no more than speculate on it may have been.

Near Manchester, in Worsley, stands Wardley Hall, whose legend says that the place will remain forever peaceful – providing the skull of Roger Downe remains there. The Downes were a prominent family who owned the Hall in the late 1600's, and Roger, so the story goes, was quite a rake. He was said to have spent a good deal of his time in London, drinking and whoring his evenings away. He was also hot-tempered, to put it mildly, and often involved in many a violent swordfight. Unfortunately for him, one evening he picked a quarrel with a man who was a far better swordsman than he. He lost his life on London Bridge, his opponent dispatching him by simply slicing off his head, which spun through the air and finally splashed into the dark waters of the Thames below.

Somehow his head, decomposed to a skull, was retrieved and sent home to Wardley Hall. His distressed sister decided to honour her brother with a proper Christian burial and set about making all the necessary arrangements. However, it seems a proper burial did nothing to lay Downe's violent spirit to rest, for during the night after the service, Wardley Hall was lashed by such terrible storms that all the inhabitants feared for their safety . . . and the next morning, Roger Downe's skull was discovered on the stairs, grinning in that unpleasant way that skulls do.

The skull was hurriedly reburied, but that night the storms returned and the next morning, so did the skull. Despite this daunting re-appearance, one more attempt was made at burying the skull for good and all, but yet again there were storms – and yet again, by morning, the skull was found back inside the Hall. Understandably, the family felt it would be safer to allow the skull to stay in the house for ever. And so the legend grew up that should the skull be removed from its chosen resting place, dire events would overtake Wardley Hall.

The skull of Father Ambrose in its resting place at Wardley Hall.

That's the legend – and the reality? It's slightly tamer – but only slightly. First we must set the record straight regarding Roger Downe, who was so maligned by this story. He was not a wild rake at all, but a barrister, who was also vice-chancellor of Cheshire and an MP. He lived to the good age of fifty seven, when he and his wife died within a few days of each other, probably the victims of a virus which was sweeping the country at the time. His coffin was actually opened in 1799 – for what reason is not clear – and his head was found to be still very much attached to his body.

As for the skull in Wardley Hall, it's real owner might well have been a Catholic priest, Father Ambrose Barlow, from nearby Barlow Hall. In the mid-1600's, this was a dangerous vocation to pursue. England was in the turmoil of the civil war, and adherents to the 'Old Religion' were persecuted wherever they were found. Large parts of Yorkshire and Lancashire were still Catholic, however, and many of the great houses in the north concealed cunningly constructed 'Priest Holes'. But the hiding place of father Ambrose was betrayed, and he was seized by Cromwell's soldiers and brought before the Assizes at Lancaster Castle. Refusing to recant, Father Ambrose was hung, drawn and quartered in September 1641. His head was believed to have been sent secretly to Wardley Hall where it remains today.

So where did the story about Roger Downes, come from? It is thought that the Downes family put the story about in order to avoid any suspicion of being Catholic sympathisers. But whatever the source of the story, the skull is real enough; it can be seen by all visitors to the Hall, residing in a specially made recess at the top of the staircase. The skull is said to dislike being moved from the house. Once it suffered the indignity of being flung into the moat – and when it became obvious after weeks of furious weather and unexplained crashings and bangings about the castle at night that there would be no peace without the skull in occupation, the moat had to be entirely drained to retrieve it again.

Similar tales are told about the skull of Burton Agnes Hall, which stands on the southern edge of the Yorkshire Wolds, overlooking Holderness. This skull story is unusual, in that whilst most 'haunted skulls' are male, this skull belonged to a woman. Burton Agnes Hall dates back to the twelfth century, but most of the building we know today was completed around 1610 by Sir Henry Griffiths, a very important man during the reign of James I, and a member of the Council for the North. Sir Henry had three daughters, and it is the youngest of these daughters, Anne, around whom this skull story revolves.

Burton Agnes Hall, the resting place of 'Awd Nance's' skull.

Over the centuries, Anne Griffiths has become known in Yorkshire parlance as 'Awd Nance', and her portrait can be seen in the Gallery at the Hall. One day she was returning unaccompanied from a visit to her friends the St. Quintins, who lived in nearby Harpham, when she was set upon by a gang of footpads. The footpads must have been particularly brutal, or perhaps Anne resisted them very spiritedly, for she was badly beaten and injured. She was rescued and hurriedly taken back to Burton Agnes Hall where her wounds were tended as well as they could be, but it was clear from the beginning that she would not survive her terrible injuries for longer than a few days. Anne was a lovely young woman who loved the Hall, above everything in her life, and she hated to think she would die and have to leave it . . . so before she drew her final breath, she extracted from her sisters the extraordinary promise that her head would be preserved inside her beloved Hall.

Perhaps it is not surprising that her devastated sisters could not bring themselves to honour this horrible request – so Anne's body was duly buried, intact, at the nearby old Norman church, where she should have rested quietly for eternity. But soon after her burial, the Hall was plagued by a whole series of strange and terrifying incidents. The family heard the sounds of a disembodied voice moaning with unhappiness, and the stillness of the large house was shattered by loud bangs – which seemed to have no obvious cause. As the family still didn't seem to take the hint, the disturbances grew even worse, with doors being slammed shut in full view of Anne's sisters and parents, when no one else was around to slam them . . . Faced with events of increasing violence, and the ever-present memory of Anne's last wish, the family at last began to wonder if their beloved Anne was responsible.

Finally, there seemed little else to do about the situation – an exhumation was arranged and to the family's dismay they found that Anne's body was no longer intact – her head had mysteriously become separated from her body, and whilst the rest of her body was relatively whole, her head had putrefied into a gruesome grinning skull.

This inexplicable discovery was enough to convince the family that it would be in their best interests to comply with Anne's last wish, and her skull was consequently brought into the Hall, where it resided for a while. Thankfully for the family, all the unsettling disturbances stopped. That is, everything was quiet until a servant girl, who probably didn't understand the significance of the skull, threw it out of a window of the house, where it landed on a horse-drawn cart which happened to be passing underneath. The horses reared up to a halt and flatly refused to move any further no matter how much they were chastised, and not until the skull was lifted out of the cart would they take another step.

This small event was taken as a warning . . . the skull was given pride of place on a table in the Great Hall, and there it stayed for many years, until it was given a more permanent resting-place when it was sealed behind the Great Hall's wood-panelled walls. And there – so the legend says – it remains to this day, though no one is quite sure exactly which panel hides it. And Anne's ghost? It is said she still haunts Burton Agnes Hall, which she loved so much.

THE RADIANT BOY

Corby Castle, east of Carlisle in Cumbria, is an eighteenth century mansion, and reputedly the home of the glowing apparition of a golden-haired child, referred to as 'the Radiant Boy'. Like all such apparitions, no one in recent times has seen the boy, but there is a vivid account of a sighting recorded in the castle's manuscript volume dated 1824. The boy was seen by the well-respected Rector of Greystoke, near Penrith, who visited Corby Castle with his wife in 1803. For the purposes of this story, we shall call him Henry Atkinson and his wife, Mary. They had been invited to stay at the Castle for several days, but they were to find just one night more than enough . . .

The Reverend and his wife picked their way carefully up the dark stairway. She went first carrying the candlestick, and he followed in the dim light clutching the carriage clock. As they ascended, Mary tried hard to remember which room the servant had shown her to earlier when their luggage was taken up. She needn't have worried, as she soon found the passageway she was looking for, and gesturing to Henry, she led the way to their room.

Mary shivered as they went in. It was a cold night, and she was grateful that a fire had been made up for them in the room. She walked across the creaking floor to the fireplace and knelt down to add more wood to the blaze.

"I can believe the tales that this place is haunted," she said, as she picked up the brass poker to position the wood more carefully. "This room is terribly gloomy and sad. Even the moonlight through the window seems dimmed, as if we were seeing it through a fine mist."

"Stuff and nonsense," laughed Henry, who also had heard the stories but gave them no credence. "The talk downstairs of ghosts and spectres has unsettled you, my dear!"

Mary put on her night-clothes as fast as she could, and climbed into the bed. The pleasant glow from the fire was cheering, and Henry sat beside it for several minutes until he felt warmer. Then, intending to make a comment to Mary about another guest at dinner, he turned around – only to find Mary already fast asleep.

Henry settled himself in bed next to his wife and considered whether to go to sleep straight away. Glad of a few minutes peace, he decided instead to read the newspaper by the light of the candle. He and Mary had been kept so busy by the parish recently that he had become very out of date with the news. It had been some months since Britain had declared war on Napoleon, and all the other dinner guests had known exactly what the war situation was – he was determined to catch up on current affairs.

The dying candle sputtered and hissed in its holder and Henry jerked his head up. Realising that he had nodded off, he folded the newspaper and placed it beside the bed on the floor. There was still some light from the fire, and he lay back and closed his eyes, seeing through his eyelids the light of the flickering flames. Henry gently drifted off to sleep.

He dreamt that he was in a cart, being taken in a hurry to a sick parishioner. The road was bumpy and the cart was badly sprung so he was being thrown from side to side. With a start he woke up. He lifted his head off the pillow, blinking, trying to understand what was going on, and realised that he had merely been having an unpleasant dream. The clock downstairs struck the half hour. He guessed it must be between one and two as he knew he had not been asleep for long. He sank back on the pillows, so disturbed by his dream that he was now wide awake.

Something attracted his attention to the middle of the room –
something aglow. There was no light in the room from the window
apart from a faint chill gleam from the half-moon, and the fire was
extinguished. Yet something seemed to be glimmering in the room. As
he watched the luminescent spot, it began to grow in size and seemed
to take on some kind of shape. Then, as the shape became clearer,
standing before him was the form of a small boy, perhaps nine or ten
years of age. The light from the child was so bright it lit up the room,
and even cast shadows. He was a pretty child, dressed all in white,
with hair that shone so brightly it seemed to be made of purest gold,
carved into curling locks. For several moments the child remained
there, with an enigmatic smile on his face, staring fixedly at Henry
almost as if he knew him.

'This must be a dream,' Henry told himself, but knew it was not.
He was fully awake, and even pinched himself to make quite sure.
Then he gasped as the child, who until now had been still as a statue,
began to move. It did not walk, but slowly glided, apparently without
movement or effort, towards the chimney breast. Its purpose was
unclear as there was nothing of interest in that area, and no doorway.
Then Henry gasped again, for the child just melted into the solid
chimney breast, and as it disappeared, the radiance which filled the
room went with it. There remained only the moonlight through the
window. For quite a while he watched the chimney-breast, now quite
dark and cold, but the boy did not return.

In the morning he told Mary what he had seen during the night,
and it was clear to her that the event had affected him badly. Generally
Henry prided himself on his pragmatism, and often said he was
prepared only to believe in things that he could see with his own eyes.
Mary always found that peculiar, for she could never understand how
he reconciled this view with his unshakeable faith in God. However,

his former scepticism on the subject of ghosts had been thoroughly shaken.

Although Henry had told his wife about his experience, he refused for the moment to discuss it with anyone else. He caused Mary great embarrassment at breakfast by announcing that they would have to leave immediately, and by refusing to be drawn on the reason for their hasty departure.

Later Henry relented. He was never able to explain his experience that night in any other terms and so concluded that he had really seen the 'Radiant Boy'. In time he wrote down a full account of the events that he witnessed and contributed it to the castle archives with his blessing.

Elegant Corby Castle, haunted by the Radiant Boy.

Corby Castle is now a private residence and is no longer open to the public. The room in which the 'Radiant Boy' appeared is now a study, but is still often referred to as the 'Ghost Room'. The Boy himself remains as one of Cumbria's most enduring legends, largely due to the written testimony of the Reverend, who was so unsettled by the ghostly child he could never stay in that room again.

THE GHOST OF MR WINTER

In 1891, in the magazine *Review of Reviews* the Durham journalist W. T. Stead published an account of the ghost of Mr. Winter – and his phantom dog. Mr Stead pronounced it "one of the most thrilling of a series of ghostly anecdotes." It had come to light when the Society for Psychical Research undertook a nation-wide census with the aim of discovering to what extent hallucinations were common amongst the general population. W. T. Stead had assisted the Society by distributing the many thousands of the census forms through his magazine, and some very interesting information was gathered as a result, including this tale.

The scene was the North Road Railway Station, in Darlington. In 1890, the station was busy enough to have a full-time night-watchman, Mr Jimmy Durham. He had worked there for fifteen years, and on the night in question he certainly didn't have ghosts on his mind. It was three weeks before Christmas, and Jimmy had been on watch outdoors in the wet and freezing weather for some time. All he could think about was how long he could endure the cold before escaping back indoors.

At about midnight, he could stand it no longer, and went inside the station. He went down to the porters' cellar where there was a cosy fire – at last he could eat and have a cup of tea. He had been outside for so long that he found the room rather hot, so he took off his overcoat, then sat at the bench to turn up the gas light. As he did so he was startled to see the figure of a large man with a big black retriever in the doorway to the adjacent coal house.

Jimmy, being a night-watchman, immediately assumed that the man was an intruder, up to no good. The two men eyed each other, and then the intruder lunged at Jimmy – he flinched as the man struck him, but felt no pain. In fact the fist seemed to go straight through him . . . By reflex, he punched the man back, but his fist passed straight through his chin and connected instead with the fireplace, skinning his knuckles.

Although Jimmy's punch made no physical impression, it did seem to have an effect on his assailant, for he fell backwards into the fireplace with a strange, unearthly squeal. The black retriever attacked next, gripping Jimmy by the leg. Jimmy definitely felt those teeth and his leg was badly hurt – although later he was amazed to find that there were no teethmarks or bruising where he had been bitten. As Jimmy was trying to fight off the retriever, the man began to recover – he called the dog off by making a sort of clicking sound with his tongue, and both he and the dog retreated back through the door into the coal house.

Jimmy feverishly lit his lantern and followed them into the room, but he could find no trace of them – which caused him great perplexity for there was no other means of entry or exit from the coal cellar.

Of course, many people were sceptical about Jimmy's strange experience and suggested that he might simply have fallen asleep and had some kind of nightmare. No one could offer any explanation as to who the man with his dog might have been, or why they would have been haunting the place in such a way. Then, some time later, the story was heard by the great Edward Pease, the "father of the railways" who had originated the Stockton and Darlington Railway with George Stephenson. He listened intently to the description of the man, who was apparently wearing a Scottish cap, and a cutaway coat, which had a stand up collar with gilt buttons.

Edward Pease found that this description reminded him strongly of a certain railway clerk he knew of – a man by the name of Winter, who had committed suicide by shooting himself on that very station. In order not to shock the passengers, his body had been hurriedly dragged downstairs and was temporarily laid out in the coal cellar – the very place to which the apparition had retreated after his fight with Jimmy Durham.

At this juncture, the story was sent to the Society for Psychical Research (SPR) who queried Jimmy Durham's reliability as a witness. This was not as unfair as it might have seemed, for time had passed before Edward Pease was able to provide an identity for the ghost, and the SPR were well aware of how much these tales can change, even over a few days. However, Jimmy's impeccable reliability was confirmed when a local churchman, the Revd. Henry Kendal, testified that Jimmy was a teetotaller, of good character and a regular attender at his church. Jimmy swore that he had not previously heard the story of Winter's suicide, and even if he had, the Reverend's statement made it clear that it would have been completely out of character for Jimmy to have made up a tale about seeing the ghost. Even so, after all this time, it's difficult to be sure that Jimmy didn't just fall asleep and have a bad dream.

The North Road Station languished for many years as a vandalised halt on the Darlington to Shildon branch line. In 1975, it was restored and is now a very attractive railway museum, the pride of Darlington town. The prospective ghost hunter will be pleased to know that the cellar is preserved and still contains the fireplace and the coal cellar where Jimmy Durham had his fight.

Since 1890 things have been less exciting there, at least from our point of view. There have been no further fights or sightings of ethereal visitors, but there have been a number of newspaper reports of unexplained incidents. Alarm systems have been known to go off unexpectedly and footfalls heard when there is no obvious cause.

Overnight ghost-watching vigils have also taken place in the restored building, and we are told that the place can be very eerie at night especially when the cold wind rushes through the roof timbers. However, the only really exciting event at a ghost-hunt was when the Mayor of Darlington reported a little puddle of water which appeared on the floor. He speculated that it might be from the spectre of Mr. Winter's dog – but we suspect that his report was not entirely serious!

Snow-covered Darlington Station as it would have been in Mr Winter's day.

SPECTRES IN STUDIO TWO

There are many stories about haunted radio stations, but one of the most interesting tales we have collected is not about a ghost at all; it's about a precognitive dream. Radio Durham was opened in 1968 and was one of the first local radio stations. In 1972, it looked as if the station might have to close, and although the rumours said that the staff would be able to move to another station in Carlisle, there was a lot of uncertainty.

Joanne Green was a free-lancer who sometimes worked for the station, and during this stressful period she had a vivid dream in which she was working in the radio station's *new* offices. She saw that the offices were very close to an enormous aerial mast. Imagine how she felt, some months later, when the staff moved to their new offices and studios in Carlisle. They were on the top floor of an office block, directly opposite a British Telecom microwave mast, which is about 200 feet high . . .

Further south, Radio Sheffield has its home in an enormous old Victorian building which has a very colourful history. The house was built in 1871, in an area which was largely occupied by prominent Sheffield industrialists. Just before the war it served as a small hotel and during the war it was used as a billet for those who operated the barrage balloons. It also served as offices for the Red Cross. After the war it was used by the Inland Revenue and then the Fire Brigade, until in 1966 Radio Sheffield took it over. They also inherited the ghost of a young girl, who is sometimes seen standing at the top of the stairs, just behind the reception area.

The legend is that the girl was a maid who worked in the house when it was a private home, and who lost her life in tragic circumstances. Exactly what those circumstances were seems to vary according to who's telling the tale. But the most frequently reported version is that she committed suicide after being jilted by the local police constable who had been her escort for several months. Other reports say that she discovered she was pregnant, and that her lover pushed her from the top of the stairs in a fit of anger. She is rarely seen these days; no one who currently works at Radio Sheffield has had a hint of her, but the story is a different one at Radio Leeds . . .

Since the 1930's, the building which houses Radio Leeds has been rumoured to be haunted by a Grey Lady. She is most often seen around Studio 2, in a dress which has no colour, just shades of black and grey. She is said to move across the gallery into the studio, with her feet a few inches off the ground. Apart from the sightings of the Grey Lady, there have been other incidents reported. One receptionist who worked there in the late 1970's stated that she was in the rest-room talking on the telephone and making a brew when something really odd happened to the kettle. The kettle lid turned around by itself, flew off the kettle and shot across the room, and landed with a clang in the sink, on the other side of the room. Not surprisingly, the receptionist swore she would never set foot in that room again!

Back across the Pennines, a few presenters and technicians at Radio Lancashire were quietly rather pleased when the station moved to its new site a few years ago. The old building had gathered a bit of a reputation for being a spooky place to be in the dead of night. One station assistant, Chris Yates, was sceptical when he was first told about Radio Lancashire's ghost. However, he changed his mind when something happened to him one winter's evening.

It was two in the morning, and outside the wind was howling, but Chris was unconcerned and busy with his editing job in Studio 2. He had worked through these small hours many times in the old building.

The weather outside was really appalling; although the studio was soundproofed, Chris could still faintly hear the howling gale and the accompanying creaking and rattling noises that were the normal sounds of an old building in a high wind.

After a while it seemed to Chris that the noises were getting louder, and he also realised that the noises were not coming from outside the building, but just outside the studio. The noises had escalated from small rattles and creaks to loud banging and crashing. To Chris it sounded as if someone was hitting and kicking the outside wall of his studio. The noises went on for several minutes, and Chris, who thought he had been the only person in place, was understandably frightened and wondered if the station had been broken into.

Eventually, some five or ten minutes later the noises stopped, and Chris gathered his courage to see if he could find out the cause of the noise. After a tour around the building, checking the locked doors and windows, he began to be more puzzled than frightened. Of course, he had found nobody else and there was no sign of a forced entry. But there was one odd thing, which added to his puzzlement – he distinctly remembered turning the main studio lights off, and on his tour around, he had found the lights switched on.

Chris was not the only person to have experiences in that old building. Basil Barker was editing and mixing in the same studio, Studio 2, in the early 1970's. Like Chris, Basil was alone in the building and busy working, when he began to feel uncomfortable, as if somebody was standing behind him, looking at him. In an attempt to bring some reality back to the situation, Basil turned the speakers on to listen to BBC Radio 2. Despite this the feelings got stronger and stronger – and suddenly he felt very cold. He looked up at the thick glass screen separating the studios and saw the expected double image of himself reflected back through the double glazing. He also thought he saw some movement behind his reflection . . . probably imagination, but nevertheless he went next door and checked. Of course, no one was there.

He tried to continue working, but the uncomfortable atmosphere persisted, and five minutes later he looked up at the thick window again. This time the hairs stood up on the back of his neck and a chill ran through him – his double image was there, but there was something else as well. He could see a dark shape reflected in the mirror – and the shape was standing behind him! He span around . . . and the studio was empty. At that point, Basil simply picked up the tapes he had been working on and fled the building, leaving all the lights and equipment still on, and the doors open.

We have only discussed three radio stations which have had reports of ghostly happenings – we suspect there may be many more, but it takes some courage to admit to such things. At night, when there are perhaps only one or two people in the whole station, these buildings can take on a gloomy and shadowy aspect, and become a completely different world from the usual daytime bustle.

There are of course plenty of theories about why such hauntings could occur and it is fair to say that as the buildings discussed here were all old, and with colourful histories. It would be strange if there were not any ghost stories attached to them. But let's not forget that the living people who work in these places are involved in the fast-paced medium of radio and frequently have to deal with all sorts of distressing and unpleasant issues. There are some who think that buildings can 'soak up' emotions and atmosphere, over a long period of time. Perhaps at night time when the studios are quiet, the buildings have an opportunity to let off this stored emotion . . .

THE OLDEST GHOST IN THE UK?

Skipsea Castle was an excellent example of a large motte-and-bailey castle – although nothing now remains of it but an enormous mound of earth. The mount occupies approximately one-fifth of an acre and was originally an island surrounded by the waters of Skipsea Mere. Skipsea is about seven miles south of Bridlington and a few miles east of the Wolds. It is also the site of probably the oldest ghost in the United Kingdom.

Skipsea Castle is *old*. The area of Holderness was given to Drogo de Bevrere by William the Conqueror as a gift for fighting alongside him at the Battle of Hastings in 1066. De Bevrere, described as a Flemish adventurer, was also granted the honour of marrying one of William's nieces. Drogo, who had the whole of Holderness to choose from for his seat, decided that Skipsea was the place, and accordingly built the castle for his new bride. It was said to be a most splendid building in its time.

History has no written record of why or how Drogo killed his wife, only that he did. However, there are plenty of local tales about how she was killed. The most prominent story is that Drogo blamed her for being responsible for his dwindling fortune. He had taken to drink, and with his thoughts thus muddled he came to believe that she was secretly a sorceress, who was using her spells to cause him bad luck and money problems. He decided that she must die if his fortunes were ever to recover, and so he gave her a potion in a chalice. He told her that it was a love potion, when in reality it was a deadly poison. Drogo then buried the Lady of Holderness near the castle. He told her servants that his wife was travelling to Flanders to visit her family.

Whether the plaguings of his conscience began to unsettle his mind, we don't know – but Drogo began to be haunted by the ghost of a Lady in White who carried a golden chalice in her hands – a chalice remarkably similar to that which he used to poison his wife.

Once he realised the enormity of his dreadful deed, Drogo was frightened that the stories of his wife's disappearance would get back to her uncle, William the Conqueror. He paid a hurried visit to William, on the pretext that he needed to borrow some money to take his homesick wife temporarily back to Flanders. William listened sympathetically, granted him the loan and Drogo promptly escaped overseas.

Once Drogo was gone and it became clear he was not going to return, his servants became even more suspicious of their mistress's sudden disappearance and mounted a search of the castle and its grounds. They eventually found her body, and notified William, who angrily sent out his constables and spies to try and locate the murderer. They were unsuccessful – Drogo had disappeared without trace, never to be found.

The castle and the rest of De Bevrere's lands were confiscated and given to the Lord of Albemarle, son of the Count of Champagne and husband of another of William's nieces. The hill bearing the earthworks which were once the castle is still called Albemarle Hill.

If you visit the Castle at any time, you may find yourself walking through an area which feels forbidding and gloomy, even though it is out in the open air. You may think you have happened on the spot where the Lady was buried – but there is another legend connected with this place. This legend dates from long before William's time, possibly back as far as the Danish occupation in the 7th century. It is said that a duel took place over the hand of a local maiden, and that a 'terrible incident' happened resulting in four large bare patches of earth where grass or plants would never grow. It is this area which feels so strange.

In fact, the Lady in White has been seen some distance away from Skipsea Castle itself. In John Nicholson's book *Folk Lore of East Yorkshire,* published in 1890, he tells of a article printed in the Hull Advertiser in 1818, concerning a gentleman who had been travelling along the road from Hornsea to Bridlington. As he ascended to the brow of a hill he saw a young lady dressed in white, about twenty-five yards ahead of him. Something about her seemed odd, and so he followed her, keeping his eyes on her constantly. At the bottom of the hill was a bridge crossing a small brook, and he hoped to catch her there in order to find out more about who she was, and where she was going. He watched the woman all the time, but as she approached the right turn onto the bridge, he was astonished to see her simply disappear.

The gentleman might have decided that he had imagined the whole affair, had he not recounted his experience to a lady friend. She assured him that he was not the only one to have seen the White Lady, as five years previously one of her servants had been riding along Skipsea Lane one morning when his horse suddenly bolted, nearly unseating him. On looking around to see what caused the horse to shy, he saw a 'fine lady, dressed in white, with something like a black veil'. The servant insisted the lady was of supernatural origin.

Both these occurrences happened quite close to Skipsea Castle – less than a mile away, in fact. The obvious assumption is that this is the same White Lady that so affected Drogo de Bevrere, and prompted his escape to the continent.

The White Lady, or 'Aud Molly' as she is known locally, is still said to walk by the enormous castle earthworks, although like most legends no one has seen her recently. There's also a local superstition that if stiles or fences are built which obstruct her chosen path, she will break them down, angry at any impediment to her endless walk, which has already lasted a thousand years . . . .

THE PHANTOM HITCHHIKER

There is a pretty country lane that runs as a 'B' road between two villages in a quiet corner of Humberside. It is about four miles long, and except for a sharp bend near the mid-point it is straight. Although it is narrow, cars tend to go quite fast for there is plenty of visibility.

In the process of researching this story, we travelled along the road ourselves to see what it is like. During the early evening when we arrived, it was very picturesque, with a patchwork of fields along some of its length, then a wooded section where the trees formed a leafy tunnel overhead, followed by more pretty patchwork fields.

But at night, it is completely different. Because it is far from street lights and far from the town, there is no light except for that of the car headlights, and if you are lucky, the moon. On our visit we travelled back along the road in such near-darkness. Apart from the occasional flare of light from the eyes of small animals caught in the headlamps, there is little to relieve the general impression of pitch darkness.

The local newspaper has made much of a 'phantom hitchhiker' who is rumoured to haunt this piece of country road. The local people are a little more circumspect about the story, suspecting that it has helped increase tourism to the villages connected by this four mile stretch and that's why it has been encouraged. Certainly the press cuttings contained a lot of exaggeration and imaginative reporting, but we still found them intriguing. We spent some time with people who had been quoted in the papers, and they were able to explain their versions of the stories behind the sensational newspaper reports. We collected five stories that day, and they were all fascinating, but one stood out above all of them, and this is the one we have chosen to recount here.

In late September 1993, Paul and Sarah were returning home from visiting Sarah's parents in Hull town centre. It was about midnight; they were able to gauge the time pretty accurately for they remember leaving Sarah's parents at 11.30 pm – their journey home takes about forty minutes – and they live ten minutes from the country lane.

Paul was driving, and perhaps because of this – she wouldn't say – Sarah was sitting in her preferred place in the back seat! Paul had just negotiated the tight bend halfway down the lane when he had to brake sharply to avoid a pedestrian who was trying to flag him down. Paul wound down the passenger's side window and asked what the matter was. It seemed that the man had been walking back to the village at the end of the lane, but in the darkness had tripped and fallen, spraining his ankle. Paul offered him a lift, expecting him to get in the front next to him, but instead he pulled forward the passenger seat and climbed into the back of the car, next to Sarah.

The man's insistence on sitting in the back made Paul immediately suspicious of the man, and he watched him carefully through the rear-view mirror. But he seemed well-mannered enough, and Sarah's impression of the man was that he was very polite. As he opened the door and manoeuvred himself and his injured foot into the car, he nearly sat on Sarah's walking stick, and with profuse apologies he lifted himself up and passed the stick over to her. Although he was polite, he wasn't very talkative, and he didn't say another word to either of them, but Sarah didn't find that surprising, for the village was only a few minutes away.

Paul pulled away from the bend and drove on to the village. As he entered the village he asked his passenger where he would like to be dropped – considering his injury, Paul was quite ready to drive him directly to his door. The man didn't answer, so Paul repeated himself a little more loudly, in case the man had fallen asleep. It was at this point that Sarah screamed, and Paul whipped his head round, wondering what on earth was going on in the back of the car. What he saw made him brake sharply and he lost control of the car, which went careering onto the pavement and into a garden-hedge.

People came running out of the house, irate at the damage done to their garden, but they soon stopped yelling and ran to call a doctor when they saw Paul, who had climbed out of the car and was wandering around in shock, and Sarah, still in the back of the car, screaming and screaming, unable to cope with what had just happened. The reason for her screaming, and the reason for Paul's accident, was that the passenger in the back had simply disappeared.

There have been many reports of phantom hitchhikers over the years, and there have been occasional accounts of passengers suddenly disappearing from the interior of cars, but this case was special. The stick that the hitchhiker had handed back to Sarah was white – Sarah was blind.

When recounting the story to us, Sarah made it clear that she had no reason to suspect that there was anything strange or special about the person that had shared the back seat with her. He smelt faintly of drink, which was consistent with his story of why he was walking along the lane – he had apparently spent all his money and had none left for a cab back home. He obviously had a physical presence, for when he sat down she felt the seat move, and he also picked up her stick and passed it to her.

The other thing about the story was that the car was a three-door model, so in order for the man to get out of the back of the car, the passenger seat at the front had to be tipped forward the same way it was when he had climbed in. Paul, of course, would have noticed that and Sarah, although blind, had a heightened sense of everything that was going on around her – she would certainly have noticed something like the front seat being tipped forward.

We spoke to both the doctor who treated Sarah and the resident whose hedge had been damaged in the accident. Both Paul and Sarah were well known in the village as practical, no-nonsense people, and there was no reason to suspect that they had simply made up their story. Since their experience, they have been helped by the knowledge that others have also seen the hitchhiker, whoever he may be, and whilst that doesn't explain what happened to them, at least they know they are not alone. The reported sightings all occurred within twelve months, and since then, as far as we know, no one else has seen the man, thumbing a lift, worse for drink and hobbling on his sprained ankle. We await further developments.

THE YORK MUSEUM GHOST

Not so long ago, in 1954, York Museum was the scene of a major controversy. There were articles about it in the local press, in-depth investigations and, eventually, the museum's curator resigned. The question which sparked these events was whether or not a ghost was present in the museum's library.

In October of that year, the *Yorkshire Evening Press* published an apparently verbatim account by the museum's caretaker, Mr G L Jonas, of how he first met the museum ghost. He described how, one Sunday evening, he was locking up for the night after the regular evangelical meeting which was held in one of the museum's rooms. He heard footsteps coming from an upstairs floor and went to investigate. At the top of the stairs he came across an elderly gentleman, who appeared to be slightly agitated and was talking to himself. Mr Jonas' first reaction was one of slight irritation, as he wished to lock up the museum quickly so as not to miss his bus home.

The gentleman was dressed somewhat oddly, in a frock-coat and drainpipe trousers. Mr Jonas tolerantly assumed that he was just another of the absent-minded academics which the museum library frequently served, who must have lost track of the time in his search for some book or other. He followed the stranger into the library and called out politely that the museum was about to close and it was time to leave.

The old man didn't seem to hear him – he was too busily engaged in pulling books from the shelves, obviously searching for a specific title, muttering to himself, 'I must find it – I must find it.' Thinking the gentleman must be slightly deaf, Jonas stretched out his hand to attract his attention . . . and then all thoughts of catching the bus left him. His visitor simply disappeared in front of his eyes. The book he had been holding, a copy of *Antiquities and Curiosities of the Church*, edited and published by William Andrews in 1896, crashed onto the floor.

When Mr Jonas had pulled himself together, he reported what had happened to the museum's curator, Mr Willmot, who was very interested by his account. He accompanied Mr Jonas into the library on several Sunday evenings, in the hope of catching a glimpse of the strange visitor. Unfortunately Mr Willmot never saw anything.

The weeks passed, and Mr Jonas claimed that he was still experiencing sightings of the old man in the museum. There seemed to be a pattern to these appearances, in that they occurred every four weeks, after the same Sunday evangelical meeting. A month after the first sighting, Mr Jonas said he had seen the gentleman again, and this time the apparition had passed into the library through a closed door. On this occasion, however, no books were disturbed.

Four weeks later, Mr Jonas was accompanied by two colleagues, and this time a thud echoed around the empty library. There, on the floor between the shelves, lay open the same book he had seen before: *Antiquities and Curiosities of the Church*. Its pages were still slowly fluttering over after the fall, but there was no one else to be seen.

A month later it was mid December. News of the apparition had spread, and several people were assembled in the library that Sunday evening waiting for something to happen. A reporter was present, and also Mr Jonas' elder brother, and even his GP – although whether he was there out of curiosity or in case any witness required medical attention afterwards, wasn't clear . . .

All the assembled held their breath, as there came the sound of a book being pulled from a shelf . . . and then a thud. The same book as before was found on the floor, and again the pages were still turning as the witnesses reached it. Mr Jonas' brother claimed to have actually witnessed the book move off the shelf. He described it as 'moving away from the shelf and the falling to the ground at a speed slower than normal'.

By this time, the affair had created considerable interest in the press, and many column inches were devoted to discussing the pros and cons of the existence of such phenomena, whilst the tabloids concentrated on sensationalising the subject beyond recognition.

It was at this point that the controversy began. The York Museum was owned by the very respectable Yorkshire Philosophical Society, who were growing uncomfortable with the goings-on and disturbed by the unexpected and inaccurate publicity surrounding the case. When their Chairman, Mr Harrowell, expressed their deep concern to the Museum's Curator, Mr Willmot, he responded that he also was unhappy – unhappy with the scepticism and lack of sympathy shown by Mr Harrowell. He offered his resignation, and it was accepted without too many protestations of regret.

Despite the wild publicity – and, we suspect, with a great deal of reluctance, the Yorkshire Philosophical Society did allow a further investigation of the case, which took place on the 7th of February the following year. This time the investigators included members of the Society for Psychical Research (SPR). The investigation was largely fruitless, although one of the investigators, Mr Jonas' brother, did claim to see a 'disembodied white hand'. A further investigation was held four weeks later, but again nothing of any interest was reported.

So what did happen at the York Museum and its library? Certainly there was far less paranormal activity than was suggested by the flurry of contemporary newspaper reports. A detailed account of the occurrences is to be found in the book *Four Modern Ghosts*, co-written in 1958 by the late Trevor Hall, who was one of the SPR investigators involved in the case. Mr Hall concludes that the movement of the book on later occasions was due to human intervention, and not by ghosts – most likely a nylon thread was used to pull the book out of the shelf.

But whilst Mr Hall expressed his concern about later aspects of this case, he admits that there is no reason to suspect that Mr Jonas was lying about his very first experience when he saw the elderly gentleman in the eccentric clothing searching for a book – which later fell on the floor. There is also no reason to suspect the later witnesses, including Mr Jonas' brother, of trickery when they claimed to hear and see the book leave the shelf and fall to the floor.

It often happens – and many would say it is entirely unsurprising that this is so – that when a particularly sceptical person is present during a vigil or an experiment into the paranormal, such happenings are rare. One explanation offered by investigators is that such sceptical people have the ability to suppress paranormal phenomena – although the sceptic would reply that this proves that what is perceived as 'paranormal' is nothing but the workings of the credulous mind.

It's also interesting that the interval between the first and last reported incident is somewhere around six months, because such a period is known to be a 'typical' length of time for the duration of a poltergeist-type haunting. But whether or not anything paranormal did actually happen, the press certainly made the most of the opportunity to fill their pages; the SPR contingent left the museum after their examination to be faced with a couple of dozen reporters eager for a good story – they must have been sadly disappointed.

So what really did happen at York Museum? Mr Jonas undoubtedly saw a poor old gentleman distractedly searching for a beloved book in the library that Sunday evening. The book, *Antiquities and Curiosities of the Church*, was one of a number of volumes left to the library by the late Edward Wooler of Darlington, and the style of clothes would suggest that it may have been Edward Wooler himself who was seen that first Sunday evening. The question which no one has attempted to answer, and which we find almost as interesting, is; *why* was he searching for this particular book so avidly? Why was he seen and heard to be muttering 'I must find it – I must find it!' What did it contain that he was so unwilling to leave behind?

HUNTING FOR THE GHOST
OF LEEDS CROWN COURT

It will now be apparent to our readers that tales about ghosts have a habit of changing as time goes on – one has only to look at the legendary 'White Lady' reports which abound in hundreds of locations nation-wide. Ask any five people to relate the legend and they will give you five different versions. When it comes to a ghost's reason for haunting, the stories are often no more than logical suggestions, without any factual basis. The same applies to modern-day occurrences, and it's important to regard any report of a ghost with a healthy scepticism until it has been thoroughly checked out. There may be any number of possible explanations for something which appears to be paranormal, and it's important to look at all the 'normal' possibilities before opting for a 'paranormal' diagnosis. It's also important to get the facts straight before you start your research . . . the following story will illustrate exactly what we mean.

When we heard of a ghost at Leeds Crown Court, we were immediately interested. The news item, which was published in May 1994, claimed that a mysterious White Lady had been seen in the court building and also in the underground carpark. Several people, including a female cleaner and a male security guard, claimed to have seen the White Lady on several occasions, and mentioned that she appeared to glide along rather than walk.

Many reasons for her appearance were suggested, but the most popular was that she may have been a victim of murder, haunting the building because her killer was not brought to justice – or, alternatively, she could have been a woman who was wrongly convicted and then died in prison. It was also mentioned, evocatively, that the building stands on the site of a nineteenth century graveyard.

This was certainly an intriguing story. We discovered that the court building was only built in 1981, and so, clearly, the White Lady could not be connected with the court itself. Her whole appearance would suggest that she had lived a very long time ago. The next step was to pay a visit to Leeds Library, and research the history of the site, looking specifically for the graveyard. We found that old maps clearly showed the squarish block of land in question and we were quickly able to build up a picture of how the area had developed. In 1815 it was still open land and had been so for centuries. A map from a few years later, in 1847, showed that a small group of terraced houses had grown up on one corner of the block. By 1893, the terraced houses had been joined by a clothing factory to the rear and a police station on the opposite corner. On the site of the court building itself, a fire station was opened in 1883, and remained there until 1974, when it was closed, demolished and the court built in its place. So where was the graveyard mentioned in the newspaper article?

In fact, the only graveyard in the vicinity turned out to be a few hundred yards from the site of the new court building; not underneath it, as the article had suggested. Oxford Place Chapel, on a plot adjacent to the court, was opened in 1835, and a graveyard was established in front of it. But as years passed the graveyard was disused and is now buried under the main road, definitely not under the court building itself.

Having done a little research, it was time to approach the people concerned, and this is where we found the next discrepancies. The article claimed that the ghost had been seen by a female cleaner, and a male security guard. In fact, they were a *male* cleaner and *female* security guard. And they didn't see a White Lady at all – they saw 'an elderly man in an ordinary grey suit'. One can understand the wish to change names and other details to protect the innocent, but this is the first time we've come across a ghost who has been afforded the privilege of anonymity to this extent . . .

It transpires that the article was instigated by the Court's own press office, and their alteration of the salient details is entirely legitimate – indeed, coverings-up of the truth is common in such news reports and we also use pseudonyms and change details where necessary. Only by checking the facts carefully can we be sure of what really happened. So, without mentioning names, the facts are as follows!

The security guard (female) saw an elderly gentleman walking through the door of a certain courtroom. Because of her training, her immediate instinct was to follow the man – she needed to know who he was and exactly why he was there. She opened the door and went through to the jury waiting area – and found there was no one there at all. There was nowhere the chap could have gone. Only then did it really register that the man had walked through the door into this room *without opening it first.*

Since then, the security guard has seen the man around the courtroom four or five times. She describes him as an elderly man, slightly balding, wearing a plain dark grey suit. His suit is not noticeably old-fashioned; it's just an ordinary suit, in fact the man himself looks completely ordinary, apart from being 'very white in the face'. Usually he is seen crouching in a corner outside the courtroom – he's there until the guard opens up the courtroom, and then he's gone.

It would be easy to claim that our security guard, despite her training, is letting her imagination run away with her. We could point out that it's simple to see shapes in dark shadowy corners, particularly in a place like a courtroom which of necessity has a sombre and serious atmosphere. But she is not the only one to have seen the man in a dark grey suit. He has also been seen by a fellow guard, who was so upset by his experience he refused to go anywhere near that particular courtroom again and made sure he was never available to open it up in the morning or lock it up at night. And downstairs, in the underground carpark, a cleaner (male) has also seen the man – and it's interesting that whilst the guard describes him as 'crouching in a corner', the cleaner says the man he sees is 'bent over'.

Our security guard laughs at the thought of being frightened by the harmless apparition. She has even given him an affectionate nickname, Fred, and if she sees him in his usual corner she greets him with a cheery, 'Morning, Fred!' She also laughs at the idea that ghosts only come out in the dark, or only at a specific time of day, or on the anniversary of a death, because from her experience that is patently untrue – she sometimes sees Fred in the morning, sometimes at teatime, and there is no pattern to the dates of his appearances.

To our minds the tale about poor Fred, crouching in the corner in his grey suit, is far more intriguing than the 'red herring' about a White Lady which was printed in the newspapers. But who is he? And why is he there? No one seems to be able to offer an explanation, despite the fact that he seems to be such a modern apparition. No one employed at the building recognises him or has heard any stories which might lead us to discovering Fred's true identity.

At one point we thought we might have a good lead to follow when we were told that the fire station, the last building to stand on the site, also had a reputation for being haunted, again by a man. It's not unknown for a ghost to be connected with a previous building on the same site, and so we spoke to an ex-fireman who had worked at the station for several years, and asked if he remembered the fire station's ghost. He told us that he had never seen the ghost himself, and didn't know anyone who had, but he recalled the rumours – they had talked about an apparition of a fireman – in full fireman's kit, not in a dark grey suit. So unless he's changed his dress to blend in with his new environment, it's unlikely to be Fred.

The haunted Crown Court at Leeds.

We have no answers to the questions about Fred's identity or his reasons for crouching in the corner . . . but it has to be said that there is still plenty of work to be done on this case. For example, there's the fact that Fred has been seen both on an upper floor and in the underground carpark. It would be interesting to find out if the first spot is directly above the second, because it has been noticed that when hauntings occur in several places in a building, the places are often on the same vertical plane. Our security guard has attempted to find out if this is the case with Fred, but says that the building is constructed in a way that makes this difficult. However, with a little patience it should be possible. It would also be interesting to talk to more ex-employees of the fire-station about the ghost – though tracking them down might take some time. It would also be quite a challenge to discover if the uniformed apparition was on the same vertical plane as the others . . . if anyone accepts these challenges, we would love to hear from them!

But before we throw this case open to other would-be investigators, we would like to repeat the one lesson we have learned from all this – and that is that you shouldn't believe everything you read in the newspapers . . .

URBAN MYTHS

In the same way that legends of all sorts probably have some factual basis, urban myths may also have some core which might at one time have been true. However, urban myths are different from the old legends because they are basically repetitions of the same story told by people across a wide geographical area. The most telling characteristic of these myths is that one never gets to hear the story from the original witness; it is always from a "friend of a friend". These stories have therefore been nicknamed 'Foafs'.

In August 1995, Melanie was invited to Radio Merseyside to talk about this book and to invite listeners to call in with their personal experiences of ghosts, with the aim of perhaps including some of them in the book. What follows is a story that we heard from one such listener, Bill Montgomery, which he first heard from his mother-in-law. She in turn first heard it from one of the secretaries at work, and the incident had happened to this secretary's son.

He was a young man in his early twenties, riding down the East Lancashire Road on a motorbike when he came across a girl by the side of the road who was hitching a lift. He stopped and asked her where she was going, and she told him she wanted to get to the Mersey Tunnel. As he was going that way he invited her to hop on the back of his bike, and he drove her to the tunnel entrance. Here he stopped again and asked her if the spot was close enough to her destination. The girl replied that she was actually going through the tunnel, to her aunt's house in Birkenhead, but she was happy to get off the bike there and hitch another lift. The lad wouldn't hear of it, as Birkenhead wasn't far out of his way. He asked her for the exact address and told her he would take her to the door.

175

At the other end of the tunnel, the lad stopped at the tollbooth. He had a terrible shock when he realised that the girl was no longer on the back of his bike. Horrified at the thought that she might have fallen off and was lying in the road somewhere inside the tunnel, he told the traffic police what had happened and they immediately headed off to check out the tunnel road. Of course the girl was not found, and the police, suspecting that the lad was playing silly games with them, suggested that they accompany him to the address the girl had given him.

They duly arrived at the house, and knocked on the door, and told the lady of the house what had happened. Yes, she said, she had a niece who answered to that description . . . *'But she died two years ago in the Mersey Tunnel – in a motorcycle accident'*.

Liverpool's Mersey Tunnel – haunted by a phantom hitchhiker?

This story was told by Mr Montgomery in good faith, as a ghost story he had heard several years ago from someone he trusted. He was aware that the tale had done the rounds of Merseyside for a few years after it apparently really happened, and it hardly needs saying that such stories change as they are retold. The oral tradition is definitely not the best way of recording such things!

Several miles north of Liverpool, Melanie was told the same story by someone in Blackburn, but it had gained a creepy twist along the way. In this version, the boy successfully dropped the girl at home, and having lent her a jacket to keep her warm, returned to the house next day to retrieve it. He was told the girl had died in a bike accident a few years before – and was even shown her grave. And there on her grave lay his jacket, neatly folded . . .

A long way south of Liverpool, Tony Wells used to live in Greenwich, and has heard the same story involving the Blackwall Tunnel. This time the address was in Wapping, on the north side. An addition to this tale is that the sound of a ghostly motorcycle is said to be heard roaring through the tunnel mouth on winter nights.

However, we may be mistaken in assuming that the 'phantom girl on a motorbike' is simply one of those urban myths which won't go away, and keeps coming back to us in a new form every few years. After all, many young women do indeed die as a result of motorbike accidents – who's to say they *don't* result in such ghosts? Who's to say that all of these stories aren't true?

While we were wondering about this point, we spoke to our friend and fellow researcher John Spencer, who has done extensive work in investigating such phantoms and myths. He directed our attention to a very similar case on the other side of the world – in South Africa! In this case an army corporal was biking to Louterwater to see his girlfriend. He came across an attractive brunette and offered her a lift, handing her a spare crash helmet and a spare earpiece for the radio he was listening to. A few miles down the road, he felt an odd bumping sensation and on looking behind him discovered his passenger was gone and the spare helmet was back on its frame.

Had our Merseyside story travelled the globe? It would be nice to think so, and it would certainly be a good ending to our story. But in fact this was one of the rare instances where an investigator actually managed to talk to the person who'd been present and had witnessed the incident. The case was investigated by Cynthia Hind, who spoke to the corporal and researched the history of the area with regard to accidents. It turned out that the corporal had picked up someone who answered the description, and was wearing the clothes of a Maria Charlotte Roux – who had been killed in an accident ten years previously. This was not just another 'foaf' story, related by a friend of a friend. It was properly researched and documented, and it's good to find one case at least where the urban myth has some background evidence – though a scientific and sensible explanation of how the phantom appeared and vanished is still just as hard to find . . . .

MURDER IN
CHESTER-LE-STREET

Whilst there are many hundreds of stories about a supposed 'message from the dead', the story that follows deserves, perhaps, to be taken seriously. Since the mid 1800's, there has been an upsurge in philosophical and scientific interest in the question of whether human consciousness can survive death. The principal focus of such investigations has been the testing of 'mediums' to discover whether such people are really receiving messages from departed spirits.

The main problem with such work is the actual content and quality of the so-called messages from the dead, which are generally of such a banal nature that not only could they have been made them up by anyone, but one is also forced to wonder why the dead bother to pass them on in the first place . . . In a test situation, a medium will know absolutely nothing about his or her 'sitter' until the test itself, thereby eliminating any chance of the medium having done a quiet bit of prior research. But there is good evidence that mediums have a well-developed ability to pick up facts about a person by observation and by reading body language. Add to this the further complication that there is good evidence to show mediums may be gleaning knowledge from their 'sitter' by unconsciously using some form of telepathy. When this is all taken into account, it is difficult to prove that the messages are actually coming from 'the other side'.

As evidence that the messages are indeed coming from the spirits of the deceased, the only kind of information which deserves close scrutiny is that which is totally unknown to the people at the sitting beforehand, and which can only be verified by checking. Such instances are rare. As investigators, what interests us most are the spontaneous cases where people who do not claim to be mediums nevertheless receive a message under circumstances which suggest that it has come from 'someone on the other side', and which later turns out to be a message of special significance.

The content of the 'message' in this story turned out to have such a special significance that in a subsequent court case it formed a large part of the case for the prosecution! The episode happened over three and a half centuries ago in Durham, and was originally reported in Surtee's *History of Durham*.

Chester-le-Street is a small village in County Durham. In 1631, a mill owner by the name of James Graham was walking down the stairs in the mill when he was confronted by the sight of a young woman standing before him on the stairs. He was shocked by her condition – her hair was a matted mess, soaked with blood from five clear wounds on her head. Such a sight would have been horrifying enough, but James Graham was even more shocked when the woman spoke to him, and explained that she was dead . . . She told him the entire circumstances of her death, and before she disappeared she pleaded with him to report the facts of her murder to the authorities.

Graham was left to think the whole thing over. The spectre had told him that she had been murdered by a man called Sharp, by being hit repeatedly with a pick, and her body then thrown into a coalpit. How could he tell anyone about this? He would face ridicule, but there was also a greater risk – if he were to tell anyone about the young woman, and how she had been killed, and where her body was concealed, and if it was all true . . . they might well think he was the murderer himself. How else could he have known such things?

However, the woman appeared to him twice more, and repeated her story, and her pleadings. There was no telling how often she would return to haunt him unless he did something – and if the story did turn out to be true, he would never forgive himself. So, at last, James Graham did go to the authorities. Perhaps it was his very reluctance to tell the story in the first place that convinced them that he was telling the truth, and not fabricating a complicated story to implicate someone else for a murder he had committed himself. In any event, the authorities took him seriously. They listened to his description of the girl's murder, which had happened on the moor, and that her body had been thrown into a nearby coalpit, whilst her bloodstained clothes and the murder weapon had been hidden under a bank. They launched an investigation – and found the body in the pit, and the clothes and the pick exactly where they had been told it would be.

As the case progressed, the full story of the murder came out. The dead girl's name was Anne Walker, and until recently she had lived with a widower by the name of Walker, in Chester-le-Street. (Their shared surname was coincidental; they were not related.) Anne had worked for Walker as a servant, but as time passed the widower had found the young girl's proximity too tempting and an affair was kindled between them. The inevitable day came when Anne discovered that she was pregnant. Walker had no sympathy for her plight and wanted nothing more to do with her. She was quickly dispatched to stay with a friend of his, a collier named Mark Sharp. It was Sharp who had murdered her, either on the instructions of Walker or with his approval.

On the strength of this evidence, Walker and Sharp were arrested and charged with murder, and tried before Judge Davenport at Durham Court in the August of 1631. James Graham appeared as a witness for the prosecution, and told the court that he had seen the ghost of Anne Walker, and that from her lips he had heard the names of her murderers, and the circumstances of her death. Walker and Sharp were found to be guilty, condemned to death, and later executed.

So, was James Graham a medium? As far as we know, he did not claim to have any special powers. As far as we know, he only had this one experience during his whole life. Or perhaps he did have others and chose not to talk about them, until this one horrific episode which demanded his attention and involvement.

Today there are many mediums who have claimed that their contact with the dead has helped the police force to catch the perpetrators of murders and other terrible deeds, but in fact there are few – if any – cases where the police would agree that the evidence given by the medium was directly responsible for an arrest. More often the medium has sensed certain details about the murder which are accurate and unknown to the general public, and although this is remarkable, it is not quite remarkable enough. One has only to look at the files of reports from mediums during massive murder hunts like the one concerning the Yorkshire Ripper to see that many of the so-called 'messages from the dead' were misleading, or entirely wrong, and in some cases a sad waste of police time and money.

The case of James Graham and Anne Walker, however, is in a different league. If it were not for James' courage in reporting his experience to the authorities, the ghost of Anne Walker might still be haunting now, yet another White Lady, unable to rest until justice was done.

THE MYSTERY OF WITCHWOOD
A WARNING AGAINST UNGROUNDED SPECULATION

One last story . . .

Running between the Lancashire towns of St. Annes and Lytham is a long narrow tract of woodland which in 1974 was designated a protected site by the Duke of Edinburgh. The trees of this densely wooded area are all protected by preservation orders, and the wood itself is cared for by the Lytham St Annes Civic Society. Access is only allowed to those on foot. The place is popular with local people and their dogs. It is such a lovely site that even people from further afield pay regular visits there to watch the changing course of nature through the seasons.

The wood is bordered by a busy main road and a railway line on one side and houses on the other. But as you walk through the trees, the houses disappear from view, the traffic-noise fades away, and all that is left is the sense of the peace and mystery which comes from being surrounded by living things. Bird-song abounds as the wood is home to dozens of species. These include great-tits and coal-tits, willow-warblers, wrens and woodpeckers, all benefiting from the cover provided by the oak, birch and willow trees. They feed on the abundant insect life to be found in the hawthorn and brambles.

If you visit the wood at any time, you may stumble upon the reason this place is called 'Witchwood'. Buried somewhere in the undergrowth is a marker stone, a gravestone barely three feet high, which bears an inscription which may send a shiver down the spine:

'The Witch – Died Jan 5th, 1888.'

It's difficult to describe the exact location of the stone. As the bramble-bushes and wild flowers cover the ground from year to year, so the stone seems to shift mysteriously from place to place. Certainly every time the authors of this book have tried to find the stone, they have to search the area very carefully.

The day the accompanying photograph was taken it was noticed that while brambles grew profusely around and behind the gravestone, nothing at all grew over the grave itself . . . and directly in front of the stone lay a little posy of wild flowers.

So who was 'The Witch'? And why was she buried here?

It would seem to make sense that a witch should be interred in unconsecrated ground. Though witches were, in 1888, no longer burned to death, nor drowned, they were hardly accepted members of polite Christian society. Perhaps this witch was regarded as, more or less, 'white' and beneficent . But why would anyone go to the trouble of having a proper headstone made for her grave?

For many centuries this land was owned by the influential Clifton family, who lived in nearby Lytham Hall. It is thanks to them that Lytham bears the nickname 'Leafy Lytham' for they were responsible for foresting the area. We must also thank the Cliftons for giving us Witchwood, and a potential local legend to go with it, for they buried 'The Witch' and marked her place for posterity.

'The Witch' was perhaps a much-loved member of the Clifton family who had taken to an older, wilder religion. Or perhaps she had helped the family in ways they could only *dare* to celebrate in this secret place. Had she made a league with the devil? Had she studied the Black Art in a long, dark book? Had she told her neighbours that the red cow didn't die by chance and that their rheumatism could not be reckoned among providential visitations? Had she modelled her enemies in wax and clay? Perhaps she was like those most famous of all witches, the three hags in Shakespeare's *Macbeth*:

> *When shall we three meet again?*
>> *In thunder, lightning, or in rain?*
> *When the hurly-burly's done,*
>> *When the battle's lost and won.*
> *That will be ere the set of sun.*
> *Where the place?*
> *Upon the heath.*

Alas, no. Further and accurate research reveals that the terrifying Witch of Witchwood was, in sober historical fact – a *horse* . . .

The Witch stone in Witchwood.

RECOMMENDED FURTHER READING

The following is a list of useful books about the Northern Legends and Ghosts, and a selection of further general interest.

Haunted England, Terence Whitaker (Contemporary 1987)

Lancashire Legends, John Harland & T.T. Wilkinson (1873, reprinted Llanerch 1973)

The A-Z Of British Ghosts, Peter Underwood (Chancellor 1993)

The Institute for Psychical Research – Ghostwatch, ed. Prof. Colin B.Gardner (Foulsham 1989)

Haunted Houses, Charles G. Harper (1907 reprinted Bracken 1993)

Haunted Britain, Antony D. Hippisley Coxe (BCA 1975)

Britain's Haunted Heritage, J. A. Brooks (Jarrold 1990)

Deliverance, Ed. Michael Perry (SPCK, 1987)

Ghostwatching, John Spencer & Tony Wells (Virgin, 1994, reprinted 1995)

Encyclopedia of Ghosts & Spirits, John & Anne Spencer (Headline,1992)

The Poltergeist Experience, D Scott Rogo (Aquarian Press, 1990)

The Evidence for Phantom-Hitchhikers, Michael Goss, Ed. Hilary Evans (Aquarian Press, 1987)

This House Is Haunted, Guy Lyon Playfair (Sphere, 1981)

Poltergeist, Harry Price (1945, reprinted Bracken, 1993)

The Paranormal, Brian Inglis (Guild, 1985)

CONTACT ADDRESSES

For those who may be troubled by ghost phenomena and would like advice, there are three main routes to follow. The first is to approach a national society such as Association for the Scientific Study of Anomalous Phenomena (ASSAP) or the Society for Psychical Research (SPR) both of which have a network of trained investigators who work to a rigorous code of conduct and promise confidentiality. Details of these organisations are given below.

The second method is to contact the Church of England. It has set up a network of Bishop's advisors in every diocese, who are happy to be contacted directly to discuss this type of problem. We have been assured that non-Christians are also entirely welcome to contact the advisors; everyone is given an understanding and sympathetic ear. It is rare nowadays for the Church to perform the ceremony of Exorcism when dealing with a haunting. Canon Dominic Walker of the Church of England is one of the busiest Bishop's Advisors; in the last 20 years he has seen many hundreds of cases of ghosts and hauntings, and yet has only performed four exorcisms. For more information on the Church of England's approach to the problem of ghosts, see the bibliography for details of the books *Deliverance* and *Ghostwatching*.

The third method is largely for those who are inclined towards spiritualism. Some mediums specialise in 'rescue work' – meaning rescue of the spirits, who may are haunting because they aren't aware they're dead. Rescue involves gently explaining to the spirit that they are now in another dimension, and should follow the light to 'the other side'. Such mediums are quite ordinary people, happy to sit and discuss the problem over a cup of tea.

As investigators, we have both worked with mediums who do this kind of work, and certainly in some cases it has proved to be an effective method of dealing with the problem. To locate a reputable medium, contact your local Spiritualist church, or the ISM (Institute of Spiritualist Mediums) at the address below.

We have found that many people like us are interested in the subject of the paranormal and would like to learn more about this fascinating field of study. Some even want to go out and spend nights in spooky castles to try and see if they can actually catch a ghost in its lair. In both cases, organisations like ASSAP and the SPR can help with information, study days, and even training days on how to investigate cases and conduct vigils.

Lastly, both authors of this book are accredited investigators, and would be interested in hearing of readers' experiences. We are investigators first, and writers second, so we will always treat people's experiences in the strictest confidence. We never publish stories without express permission, and always obtain agreement on the content of stories before publication.

The Association for the Scientific Study of Anomalous Phenomena

(ASSAP for short!).

Its objectives are to study in a scientific manner a wide range of anomalous phenomena, including ghosts, UFOs, and out-of-body experiences. ASSAP has a training system for investigators, who must be approved before contacting the public. ASSAP welcomes enquiries for investigation of incidents and enquiries for membership from people of all beliefs.

Address for enquiries and membership:

ASSAP, Saint Aldhelm, 20 Paul Street, Frome, Somerset BA11, 1DX.

Contact Hugh Pincott Tel: 01373 451777.

The Society for Psychical Research (SPR)

Founded in 1882, its purpose is to examine without prejudice and in a scientific manner those faculties of man which appear to be inexplicable. Welcomes enquiries from interested people of all beliefs.
Address for enquiries and membership:
49 Marloes Road, London, W8 6LA. Tel: 0171 937 8984.

The Institute of Spiritualist Mediums

The Institute exists to advance the religion and religious philosophy of Spiritualism. It provides training courses for those interested in mediumship; for those who wish to attend medium's circles it will provide lists of local registered mediums, including rescue mediums.
Address for enquiries and membership: 27 Honeyden Road, Sidcup, Kent, DA14, 5LX Tel: 0181 300 7260.

The Authors

Can be contacted via the publishers: Broadcast Books, 4 Cotham Vale, Bristol, BS6 6HR Tel: 0117 973 2010 Fax: 0117 9741293

Church of England Bishop's Advisors

Otherwise known as Deliverance Ministers. Can be contacted by looking up any local C of E church in the phone book and asking for the number of the nearest diocese Bishop's office. For more information about the Church of England's approach to ghosts and exorcism, see the book *Deliverance,* mentioned in the reading list.

The Roman Catholic Church also advises on possible cases of supernatural disturbances.